Christ,
and Christian Experience in
the Tabernacle

Together With Some Teaching Upon
the Priesthood, Offerings, Feasts, Etc.

by

Charles T. Potter

First Fruits Press
Wilmore, Kentucky
c2018

ISBN: 9781621718420 (print), 9781621718437 (digital), 9781621718444 (kindle)

Christ and Christian Experience in the Tabernacle: Together with Some Teachings Upon the Priesthood, Offerings, Feasts, etc.
By Charles T. Potter.
First Fruits Press, © 2018
Digital version at
http://place.asburyseminary.edu/firstfruitsheritagematerial/156

Potter, Charles T.
    Christ and Christian Experience in the Tabernacle: Together with Some Teachings Upon the Priesthood, Offerings, Feasts, etc. / by Charles T. Potter. Wilmore, KY: First Fruits Press, ©2018.

    159 pages ; cm.

    Reprint. Previously published: Cincinnati, Ohio : Office of God's Revivalist, 1903.
    ISBN: 9781621718420 (pbk.)

    1. Worship in the Bible. 2. Tabernacle.   I. Title.

BM654.P677 2018

Cover design by Jon Ramsay

asburyseminary.edu
800.2ASBURY
204 North Lexington Avenue
Wilmore, Kentucky 40390

First Fruits
THE ACADEMIC OPEN PRESS OF ASBURY SEMINARY

First Fruits Press

The Academic Open Press of Asbury Theological Seminary

204 N. Lexington Ave., Wilmore, KY 40390

859-858-2236

first.fruits@asburyseminary.edu

asbury.to/firstfruits

CAPTAIN CHARLES T. POTTER.

CHRIST,

AND

Christian Experience in the Tabernacle.

TOGETHER WITH SOME TEACHING UPON
THE PRIESTHOOD, OFFERINGS,
FEASTS, ETC.

BY

CHARLES T. POTTER.

OFFICE OF GOD'S REVIVALIST,
MOUNT OF BLESSINGS,   CINCINNATI, OHIO.

INTRODUCTION.

GOD has ever jealously guarded His own honor, and while He does not pass by the wise of earth He does glory in selecting instruments that would never be chosen by men. This He does "that no flesh should glory in His presence." We are living in the "last days" and in "perilous times;" "heady," "high-minded," "having a form of Godliness," and like words and expressions locate us. In the rush after knowledge, and the tendency to bow down to intellectuality, we forget that "the foolishness of God is wiser than men, and the weakness of God is stronger than men." "For the wisdom of this world is foolishness with God."

The learned Paul was careful to so preach that the faith of his hearers "should not stand in the wisdom of men." Years ago God laid His hand upon a poor, ignorant, sinful fisherman; and a few years afterwards sanctified him wholly. Feeling the call of God to work for the salvation of the lost, he set about the study of the Bible, especially the Old Testament. For years, as he followed his occupation, he pored over the Word, searching as for hid treasures. Years have been spent in careful re-

search. Old libraries and second-hand bookstores
have been ransacked for information. The rarest
specimens and material pertaining to the Tabernacle
and its furniture have been collected from this and
foreign lands, until a fund of information has been
obtained that makes the writer an authority on this
branch of sacred study.

Finally, with a direct call from God, Charles T.
Potter left his nets to give all his time to catching
men. In halls and churches, at conventions and
camp-meetings, these sermons have been used of
God in awakening and helping many people. After
much prayer it was believed to be the mind of the
Spirit that this valuable information should be put
in a permanent form, and given a wider range of
influence. Accordingly it was arranged that these
sermons should be delivered in Providence, and from
notes (and stenographic reports) the following chapters have been compiled.

In every emergency God has His man. Brother
Potter himself, unaccustomed to prepare matter for
the press, was dependent upon some one interested
and spiritual, who could select, revise, and arrange
for publication. This part of the work was laid
upon one who was, we believe, in every way quali-
fied for the task. This he does for the glory of
God, not wishing even to be known in connection
with the book. We feel sure that under the guid-

ance of the Holy Spirit, whose aid has been constantly sought, these brothers have been enabled to put before the public a book that will prove a valuable addition to Holiness literature. From an intimate acquaintance with the author, and the one who has assisted, we hesitate not to say that they have had an eye single to God's glory. They seek neither honor nor financial gain. All profits arising from its publication have been dedicated to the spread of the gospel in foreign lands.

May the Holy Spirit, who called these sermons into being, use them to awaken a sleeping Church and a dying world! As they exalt the Lord Jesus Christ, in whom all types have their fulfillment, may believers see their privileges in Him and sinners be led to the "Lamb of God that taketh away the sin of the world!" May the truths found in this volume help to counteract the refined and subtle unbelief of the day, and exalt our great High Priest, who "by His own blood entered at once into the holy place, having obtained eternal redemption for us;" who "because He continueth ever hath an unchangable priesthood, wherefore He is able to save them to the uttermost who come unto God by Him, seeing He ever liveth to make intercession for them."

This book, carefully read and pondered, will turn our gaze from earth to heaven, inspire to a holy life and a self-sacrificing service, and prepare us to walk as "strangers and pilgrims," and to "look for Him who shall appear the second time without sin unto salvation." May God bless the book! May it prove a help to hundreds in the home land, and the proceeds from its sale bless thousands abroad!

May 4, 1903.   JOHN PENNINGTON.

TABLE OF CONTENTS.

ILLUSTRATIONS.

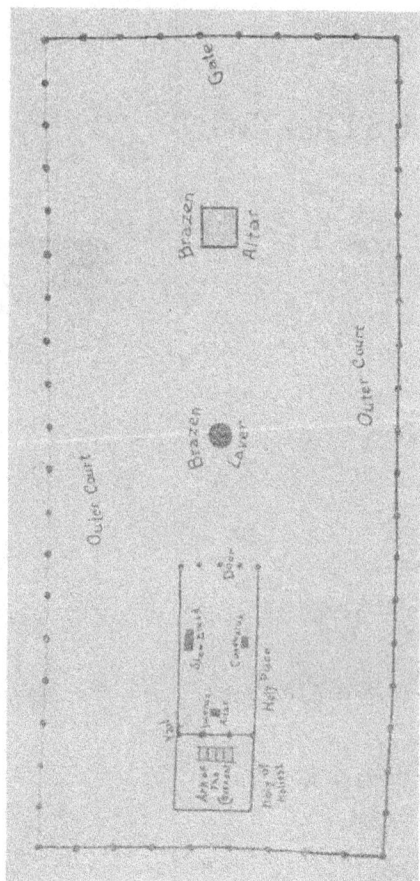

THE GROUND PLAN.

DIMENSIONS.

Outer Court, 150 feet x 75 feet.
Holy of Holiest, 15 feet x 15 feet.
Holy Place, 15 feet x 30 feet.
Sanctuary, 15 feet x 45 feet.

DIMENSIONS.

Gate, 30 feet x 7 feet 6 inches.
Door, 15 feet x 15 feet.
Vail, 15 feet x 15 feet.
Outer Court Pillars, 7 feet 6 inches high.

Christ and Christian Experience in the Tabernacle.

CHAPTER I.

MOSES, AND THE ASCENT INTO THE MOUNT.

BEFORE beginning the study of the Tabernacle, it seems right to notice the man to whom God revealed His plan regarding it. His name was Moses. He was of Levitical parentage. His father's name was Amram (meaning people of the exalted), his mother's name was Jochebed (meaning whose glory is Jehovah). The child was "a proper child." When the decree was made to cast into the river every male child that was born, he was hid of his *parents*, showing their *united* faith. When he was put in the ark in the river Nile, Miriam (his sister) stood afar off to watch what would be done with him. And Pharaoh's daughter beheld him and the babe wept, and the weeping was of the Lord. And she had pity upon him and said, "This is one of the Hebrew's children. And she called his name Moses, "drawn out," for she said,

"I drew him out of the water." And Miriam (play-
ing the part of intercessor) brought to Pharaoh's
daughter the child's own mother, and Pharaoh's
daughter said, "Take this child away and nurse it
for me, and I will give thee thy wages." What a
sermon there is in this text, Take *this child* AWAY—
away from Egyptian influences, and *I will pay thee
wages!* He became a mighty man in word and
deed, and refused to be called the son of Pharaoh's
daughter, *esteeming** the reproach of Christ greater
riches than the treasures in Egypt. But he undertook the leadership *out of order;* viz., by force of
arms; he slew an Egyptian and rebuked the Israelite, and fled (when it was discovered) to the wilderness. His life was divided into three periods of
forty years each; the first forty he was in Egypt,
the second he was in the wilderness, and the third
he was leading the children of Israel through the
wilderness and towards the promised land. Moses
was a *resurrected* child. In this as in many
other respects he was like our Lord. (Acts iii,
22.) He died first to his natural parents; then
he died to his adopted parents and to the fact
that he was heir to the throne and to all the advan-
tages of Egyptian civilization, "choosing rather to
suffer affliction with the people of God, than to enjoy

---

* Notice the word. God help us to "esteem" like Moses! Esteeming.

the pleasures of sin for a season." Putting, as it were, a throne behind him, he became a shepherd; and every shepherd is an abomination to the Egyptians. As we become heavenly shepherds we are an abomination to the world! During his wilderness training he begat two sons; the name of the elder means "I'm a stranger here," and that of the other means "God is my helper." Moses was *eighty* years old when he was ready for service. Let the gray-haired ones take courage. It is just the time for God to use! Miriam was ninety years old when (instead of stooping!) she led the people in the gladsome dance.

At the end of the forty years spent in the desert he saw the burning bush. It was holy ground, and strong as Moses was in the natural he was there afraid, and trembled and hid himself. This mighty man, when God wanted him, became slow of speech! Aaron was given him, but he was a trouble. God then told him, "Certainly I will be with thee; and this shall be a token unto thee, that I have sent thee. When thou hast brought forth the people out of Egypt, ye shall serve God upon this mountain." And accordingly after God had delivered Israel, He called Moses up into this very mount. (Ex. xxiv.) It is not everybody that is dead enough to go up into the mount with God! Moses was now ready. Nadab, Abihu, and the seventy elders of Israel must

worship afar off. The people prove obedient, and
built altars and offered burnt-offerings and peace-
offerings, and Moses took the blood and sprinkled
it upon them, and *after the blood was sprinkled* he
went up; then also the thunderings and lightnings
stopped. These elders were suggested by Moses'
father-in-law, and were troublesome—they could not
go up. In the ascension of the mount there were
three definite stopping places. The first place (Ex.
xxiv, 10) they saw the God of Israel, and ate and
drank and had communion. There was here, as it
were, a sapphire pavement; but God gave no "pattern" here. Then Moses was called higher, and
taking Joshua, his minister, with him the glory of
the Lord stood upon Sinai (the point), and they
staid there six days (verse 16), and the seventh day
God spake out of the cloud, and Moses went into
the midst of the cloud. At the first resting-place
with the elders they had a blessed time, like one of
our modern camp-meetings; but Moses must go
higher and leave the elders behind. At the second
resting-place, where he and his minister were alone
with God, the manifestation was greater; but the
time came when he must leave even his minister
behind, and Moses alone "gat him up into the
mount." I like those words, He *gat* himself up
into the mount. How expressive it is! Upon this
third and highest point of ascension, where Moses

was alone with God, he remained forty days and forty nights. (At half-past ten some people leave the meeting-house, and if the time of prayer be long they complain of its hurting their knees! Do they not *miss the pattern?*) There comes now in the life of Moses a definite period of one hundred and twenty days, composed of three divisions of forty days each; viz., forty on the mount; forty in intercession; forty again on the mount, repairing the loss of the first tables by making the new. When Moses descended he found Joshua, who had never backslidden; but the elders had gone back. The people had taken their jewelry and made a calf. Let us have no jewelry; then we can not worship it!

They sang around this calf; but the Bible calls it *"a noise of singing."* Surely we have some singing to-day that is not in the Holy Ghost, a "noise of singing." When people are in the calf business the singing becomes *noise,* and the *eating* and drinking resembles the modern oyster-stew and bean-supper sociable. God's anger was kindled against the people. He said to Moses, "They are *thy* people." We sometimes hear of people that are converted to an evangelist to-day. But Moses reminded the Lord of His promise to Abraham, Isaac, and Israel, and became an intercessor for the people. He prays another forty days and nights, and in holy desperation says, "If not, . . . blot me, I pray

thee, out of Thy Book which Thou hast written."
O, that wordless pause! Is there anything finer outside of the life of our Lord Himself? Moses stood
in the breach. He had gotten beyond the needs of
his stomach, beyond pain of the knees, beyond life
itself, and GOD HEARD HIM. The skin of Moses'
face shone when he talked with God; but he wist it
not. So he covered his face while he talked with
man; but when he talked with God the veil was done
away. The people were made to drink the water
of their idolatry. God wants us to drink the water
of life—"Hallelujah water!" Moses so learned to
know God that he could take care of five million
people without a gun being fired. God talked to
Moses (Ex. xxxiv), and told him to clear out the
old images and altars, and drive out the Amorites
and all "ites." And God tells His holiness people
to-day, who meet in simple halls and missions, to
tear down the altars of the backslidden denomina-
tional ministers. Moses now ascends the mount
again *alone,* for forty days more. His knees, no
doubt, are callous. One of those callous spots would
save a whole city in our modern days. He had to
come down before because the people disobeyed.
When he next came down the people ran, for his face
shone.

Let us now begin our study of the Tabernacle.

We will take two texts for our leading thought—
Ex. xxv, 8: "And let them make me a sanctuary,
that I may dwell among them;" Ex. xxv, 40: "And
look that thou make them after their pattern, which
was showed thee in the mount." This was not the
Jewish tabernacle; it was *God's* tabernacle. The
word Jewish has the thought of division in it. The
Tabernacle was to be a place where God could
dwell, not visit for a time. Know ye not that your
bodies are the temples of the Holy Ghost? The
Tabernacle shows out the spiritual life of us all,
and every doctrine of the New Testament is found in
its teaching. Notice the condition we must be in
to get God's pattern! *People* have different pat-
terns; God has *one*.

I am tired sometimes, and think of going HOME.
Then I look at the Tabernacle to see if I 'm like it!
Moses saw the Tabernacle in heaven, and you and I
will see it there. But Moses had to be prepared.
I do n't read the latest things; I am reading God's
Book. It matters not what people say; but what
God says. If you do n't build by the pattern, you
will have dry spots. I got sanctified under Wesley's
teaching; but he was n't everything! After I was
converted I saw a Bible, and parts of it were un-
thumbed, and I made up my mind I would study
that part. In there was the Tabernacle! I went to

2

hear a sermon; but the Lord kept talking to me about the Tabernacle. A year and a half from that time I had it. You 'll have to get above the objections of your friends. The Tabernacle is not an ice-house; it is a spiritual house of warmth and blessing.

THE TABERNACLE.

DIMENSIONS.

Goat's Hair Covering, 45 feet x 66 feet.

Fine Linen, 42 feet x 60 feet.

CHAPTER II.

THE WILLING OFFERING.

A GREAT many people call themselves Israelites who do not know what an Israelite was. An Israelite was a soldier of God, one to whom the bondage of Egypt was hateful. We find plenty of people who profess to be Israelites, yet they do not feel the bondage of this world; but if you are a true Israelite there will be a bondage in your soul, and you will groan to God until God will come down to deliver you, and you have gone out of Egypt and gone out *free*. No man has been delivered out of Egypt who does not have something when he goes out. They *"spoiled"* the Egyptians. We ought to spoil Egypt. This is what an Israelite is! You will be so rich that others will think they need to be sanctified to God! You will have so much gold on your backs that you can hardly go along! God made a covenant that no diseases should come upon them, but he would keep them from sickness. This promise was given before the law. First *be* an Israelite; then bring an offering. This offering must be according to order—gold and silver, etc. (Ex. xxxv, 5-9.) Something fit for a sanctuary,

and for shekinah glory! God did not seek for the
unwilling to bring an offering to Him. God does
not want it. The condition of the people must be
willing-hearted, not stingy. The thought is prevalent for the ungodly person to give *himself* to the
Lord before he can come to the place where *he can
make an offering.* What is found on you, you must
give. God sees and knows what you *can* give. It
may be gold, silver, or precious stones; fine linen
or even goat's hair, spices or oil; all of these things.
God is very minute as to what they are. You might
come along and offer the Lord an offering, and He
would not take it. The offering is to be used for a
sanctuary, a place for the real worship of God.

So this offering had to be brought in a proper
condition of heart by the people who brought it.
None but willing-hearted people could bring it. A
willing offering is to pass in gold, if you have gold;
brass, if you have brass. Glory to God, we have
some one who searches us from our heads to the
soles of our feet! He sees the gold and silver, He
sees the oil and fine linen, He sees all the arrange-
ments. You can not lie to God, and a true Israelite
does not want to lie to God. This willingness of
heart is stirred up by the Spirit of the Lord. It is
not a willingness to give because you think that you
will get something from it. The heart that has been
made pure is not selfish. A heart that has been

made right God can *trust*. The offering that we are telling about will be acceptable to the Lord.

Men and women came and gave such as they had, and they laid it down before the Lord—spices and oil and goat's hair and different things. And as you see this offering laid here before God, it is like a great lumberyard. And now begins the work of those whom God had stirred up in wisdom and understanding to work all manner of fine work and embroidery, and wise-hearted women that came to spin the goat's hair. And out of this confusion of raw material given to the Lord everything comes down in God's order.

How much rough material has come! I know of a poor boy—a great fighter. Sin had done its work on him, and there was a big swelling on the side of his face. If any one wanted fun or a betting-match, they took this boy. He came into the mission one day and staid just a moment, and then suddenly he ran out of the door. But the saints of God were praying for that young man. They did not know who he was, but they prayed because they saw the marks of sin on him. Finally he came again, and ran out as before; then came again and staid longer. One time a German girl went to him and put her hand on his shoulder, and said, "God wants to save you." He broke down, and gave his heart to God. That boy commenced to pray, and a woman

who claimed to have been saved said, "Had n't you
better speak to that young man; his words and expressions are fearful." I would just as soon put
my hand on God as on him! I heard him breathe
out his soul to God in prayer, and everybody sat
stricken to hear that fighting man pray! If you
could look at his picture, you would see the look of
sin has gone out of his countenance now.

And so they came, men and women, and brought
this offering to the Lord, and everything was fixed
as He wanted; but, mind you, in the thirty-seventh
chapter of Exodus it says that after that they
brought fresh gifts every morning! There will
come a morning when new light will come upon
you, and you will reach your hand down deep in the
coffer and bring out another bag of gold. Morning
after morning they gave until the time came when
everything was all right, and the work they were
doing was all right; and when they had enough they
called what was over "stuff!" All God wants is
a sanctuary and place of worship; and all beyond
that is stuff! I found it so in my experience; all
beyond a set place of worship is stuff.

Bezaleel and Aholiab made rough things smooth
for the Tabernacle. They were "wise-hearted," not
wise-headed. God Almighty gave His orders as to
how the Tabernacle *should be built,* and upon what

conditions they might worship Him; there must be a *Tabernacle*. Praise God for the TABERNACLE!

A little thought about the linen here, though some lessons on it come later. We are not told of any one who *spun* it. *We* can not spin it! It is spun in glory, and put in you and me! You and I can perfect it, and put embroidery work on it! It says "fine linen," fine twisted thread linen. God wants to twist you, and twist you until you get where you belong, and *He* can make fine linen out of you. It is no use to try to make fine linen out of yourself. I used to try to be holy! Did you ever try to be holy?

I want now to call your attention to the fact that when Moses describes the Tabernacle in Exodus, twenty-fifth chapter, he begins with the Ark of the Testimony; but in Exodus, thirty-sixth chapter (after the first tables were broken and the new ones were made that were never broken) he begins with fine linen, thus signifying the righteousness of the saints, and contrasting, I think, the two dispensations of law and grace. After the fine linen he then takes the other three coverings, and following that the boards (signifying the individual believer), the rings and bars (which unite the individuals), then the veil and door and ark of testimony, from which point he proceeds in the same order as before.

When he began with the fine linen covering, we are to remember that *under* that covering was the precious work; everything seemed to be put in afterwards. One might look to be all right outwardly; but I would like to have God look me over, and I would like Him to look some other people over; I would like Him to blow out the bank books and trunks, and see what we have. You might say, "I have not much; I have but one half talent." He calls for that half talent. You say, "If I had a whole talent like some of you, I would." If you have any talent, you have ONE. If you have not one, you had better come to Him and get one. When I began to testify I seemed like a big fool. I would come to the front seat and look the people in the face, and finally say, "Praise the Lord!" and begin to blubber. Time after time the old devil said, "You great, big, old baby." But I told God that if He would save my soul I would testify, I would say something; it might not sound much at the outer end, but it would be an awful lot at the inner. Then God split my tongue, and I never had any trouble from that day to this. Some say, "Well, I can't speak like Mr. So-and-So, or I would." If you talk that way you will get out of the meeting-house in a few weeks! My wife gets up, and before she begins to talk her chin will commence to quiver and the tears will come; and when she gets home I tell

her how good she talked! If the Lord wants you to
blubber and cry it's all right. I have seen more salvation out of one breakdown than anything else.
I say these things because you have an offering, and
God knows all about it. It may not be the same as
some one else brought; it may not be gold or silver;
it may be "goat's hair." It is not what you do; it
is what the Divine workman does with what you
bring to Him. If they had only brought gold there
would have been too much gold, and a lack of other
things. If the *Divine workman* did not take hold,
the *beauty* in the Tabernacle would not be brought
out. They brought earrings and bracelets, they
brought all the ornaments they had. It is a blessing
to get to the place where you are willing to take your
ornaments and make an offering of them that will
glorify Him. Sometimes you do not have much.
The children of Israel never had much; they took
(and "borrowed") from the Egyptians and brought
about this Tabernacle. It was composed, therefore,
of the very material that had cost them so much of
labor and suffering when they had served these
people in cruel bondage. I know about some trials,
and so do you. Little did we dream that the work
we did when in spiritual Egypt could ever be turned
to account for God in later years!

I was nothing but a fisherman. I ran away from
school. There was nothing left of me but a little

goat's hair. Everybody seemed to put a hand to push me down. After I was converted I used to keep hens and pray in the hen-house, and the people did not like it; but the time came (when one of them was dying) that they sent for the man that prayed so loud in the hen-house! After *that* they let me alone; but tried to tell me HOW to do it! Brothers and sisters, you pay God and bring the offering that God has for you; bring what you HAVE, and it will be satisfactory to Him.

NOTE.—The value of the offering to the Lord for the building of the tabernacle was: Gold, $875,000; silver, $198,605; brass (copper) $690; total, $1,073,295. This does not include wagons and oxen (given by princes or heads of families), curtains, coverings, wood, cords, blue, purple, scarlet, fine linen, dress of high priest and sons, precious stones, spices, and oil; nor the great labor of making and putting the material together. It was a free-will offering, and gladsome service for Him. There were no salaries. It was a love service, like the slave who refused to be set free whose ear was bored with an awl. And we can bring like offerings, praise God! and He has the glory forever.

CHAPTER III.

WITHIN THE VEIL.

WE are now going into the Holy of Holies. One place where I lectured upon the Tabernacle they asked me why I commenced with this sacred spot, and I said, "Because God began in that way." He commences with the ark, and goes *down* until the high priest takes hold of us, and then He carries us *up* to God. The first part of the thirty-fifth chapter of Exodus brings out the Ark of the Testimony. How plain it is that this ark represents a human being! And that as they were to furnish the wood, and then the wood was to be covered with gold, so we furnish the NATURAL material and God works in the Divine. The gold was to be put within and without (not without and within!), inside and outside. After they overlaid it with gold, they were to put a crown around it. This betokens the GLORY there is down here, around the ark that is gold within and without. Then it speaks about cast rings made of gold, gold that had been through the crucible fire and made pure so that He could use it to represent Divinity. So many people never get any fire, and they are so stiff and cold they never

can be made into rings! Staves go through these
rings, for the ark is to be borne aloft; it is not to
be set down. In all the other pieces of furniture
the staves might be taken out; but from the ark
they were never to be withdrawn. We are then told
what is to be put in the "Ark of the Testimony."
After our natural man is covered with gold, we can
then have a testimony! O, what an awful job it is
to try to say something when you have nothing to
say! Did you ever learn a piece at home, and when
you got to the place you could not say it, and you
must say something? Alongside the testimony was
the golden pot of manna. How mysteriously this
manna fell, reminding us of the mystery of the coming of Christ to the human heart! "What is it?"
they said, and then they tasted it. There are lots
of things we know nothing about until we taste
them. "Come taste, and see that the Lord is good."
Some people are too straight and stiff to kneel down
in the place of humility, and gather the manna. If
you gather much you will have nothing over, and
if you get a little you will have enough! A man,
just out of college, once asked me how I fixed it up
to get my knowledge for preaching. I told him I
kept catching lobsters! You stay about what God
gave you to do; wash dishes, be a tool maker, and
stay with God till you hear from Him. When you

DIMENSIONS.—2 feet 8 inches high; 3 feet 6 inches long; 2 feet 8 inches wide.

hear from Him there are not devils enough in hell
to drive you out of the ministry.

Here also was the rod that was taken from
Egypt, that budded and brought forth fruit. Moses
was so meek; but by this rod God vindicated him
when the people questioned his authority. O, it is
a dreadful thing to go into the ministry without
being called of God. *Here* the earth opened its
mouth and swallowed such people up. If you will
be wholly the Lord's and be a Levite, God will write
His name on your rod. I have now no time for
ministers not called of God, who when they preach
throw out buttonhole bouquets for people to smell
of, and who fix themselves up in short pants and go
round with a golf stick. I know they are swallowed
up by the world.

These are the three testimonies God said must
be put in the ark. If you are going to be an ark,
especialy made of gold within and without, these
three things will be in your experience. This ark
was in the Holy of Holies—a place fifteen feet
square. It was covered with the fine linen covering,
and separated from *even the holy place* by the veil.

Over the Ark of the Testimony was the mercy-
seat, which was a separate piece of furniture. The
two cherubim were beaten out of the mercy-seat.
Why, these cherubim are nothing more nor less than

the work of the mercy-seat. They represent RE-
DEEMED beings. Scripture says they are "beaten
out" of the mercy-seat; their wings are spread out,
and they look towards the mercy-seat, where the
blood was sprinkled on the great day of atonement.
All of us are representatives of His mercy everywhere. This angel experience is sometimes represented by the eagle life. If you get into the Shekinah glory you will get the eagle experience. You
can starve an eagle to death, but he never dies di-
rectly through disease or old age. This eagle glory
produces the spirit of martyrdom and missions.

You find when the Israelites got away from God
and thought they had no further need of the Ark of
the Testimony, that they left it down in Shiloh. And
you can get rid of the ark if you want to. (I can
find many people that have left the ark in Shiloh.)
You might be in some meeting-house of the Philistines, the enemy of God's people, and not take the
Ark of the Testimony there! Israel did not have
the ark with them when the Philistines pitched the
battle; but they thought they would have the victory.
When the Philistines beat them, Israel said that God
denied their cause; but the real reason was that they
did not have the ark with them nor the Divine glory.
This is the reason we get defeated too! They were
defeated because they were not right. What is the
use of seeking Divine glory when you are not right?

The ark of God was taken and carried into the Philistine country, and right off there was trouble. They said they must get it out of there, and they took it to Gath. And there was trouble in Gath. Then they made a cart and some images of things, and tied the cart to two cows that had calves, and let the cows go; but those cows had the Divine Presence in them, and they went contrary to all natural inclinations. If those cows could have talked, they would no doubt have told you that they were impelled by Divine power. Down in Bethshemesh they went, where they were reaping their wheat harvest. I want to tell you it means something to have your field of wheat, for after you reap it—after wheat harvest—comes Pentecost! There must be a road for the Holy Ghost to come into the field. Take your bars down! In came these cows as quick as they could into that field. It means something to be ready for the Holy Ghost to come. They broke up the cart and killed the cows. How many would go to the harvest field if they were called, even if it meant sacrifice on your part? If you had asked those cows as they were going along where they were going, they would have said they only had one thought; viz., to go where that Divine Presence impelled them. When the Israelites got the ark back they peeped in, for they wondered if there was anything lost. So they lifted the lid, and for that action

a whole lot of them were killed. *We* must look out.
"I wonder how the *old meeting-house is getting
along?*" Any of you peeping?

Then you know they were all scattered, and they
said, "Who can stand before this holy Lord?"
Twenty years the Israelites were without the Divine
Presence; but there came a time when the people
got anxious, and they got hold of this Ark again.
David made a *new cart.* God save us from new
carts! Then they put two men, one on each side,
to *steady* it; I guess one of them must represent
the Christian Endeavor Society! David was
afraid—you need not be afraid if you are *right;*
you need not be afraid if you are with God—but
King David was afraid; so they carried it to the
house of the little fellow that lived down the lane,
to Obedeedom's house. Now, if any one don't believe in an instantaneous work of grace, you ought
to have seen the big peaches and watermelons, and
everything that came from Obedeedom's house!
The market was full of good things, all raised at
Obedeedom's! He had eight children, and they
were all "ABLE MEN" of might. Somebody up
and told David—I imagine they said something like
this: "David, come down to the market. We had
some things on the table to-day that came from
Obedeedom's; the public markets are all full of
things that came from there!" So the king com-

menced to think he wanted that. This is the way people get hungry for the Blessing. "I do n't want the old sour fruit. I am tired of rotten apples." David might have said, "I undertook it three or four times and made a failure." But Obedeedom did not make any failure. It is the one that did *not* make any failure that brought good from it. It will be such an instantaneous work that everybody will see it. David went down and got the Word of God and went to Obedeedom's house, and David found out from the Word of God that none but sanctified people should carry His Ark. He could now see how, if he had taken God's order, he could have safely brought the Ark. So now he prepares a place for it and sanctifies the place. Then the Glory of the Lord just shone around—how He likes to bring out the Glory! David then got to praising the Lord; and he praised Him with dancing, and his wife did not agree with Him, but God struck her with barrenness (how much spiritual barrenness there is to-day!), and he went right on praising the Lord. Obedeedom was an insignificant little man, but he brought out the Glory, and then the victory came! If there is ever a day when the Philistines come to you, you "look this way and that way," and when people ask which way you will go, say you will go God's way, that is, UP. People have asked me where

3

the Ark of the Covenant is now. If any one should want to dig it up to try to please a lot of skeptics, he might try to do it; but I do not need it; I have my own Ark of the Covenant. I worshiped in a place once that had no clapboards on it; it was a hard looking place, but it was glorious within. There is a completeness in the Christian life. You can recognize it by the Glory.

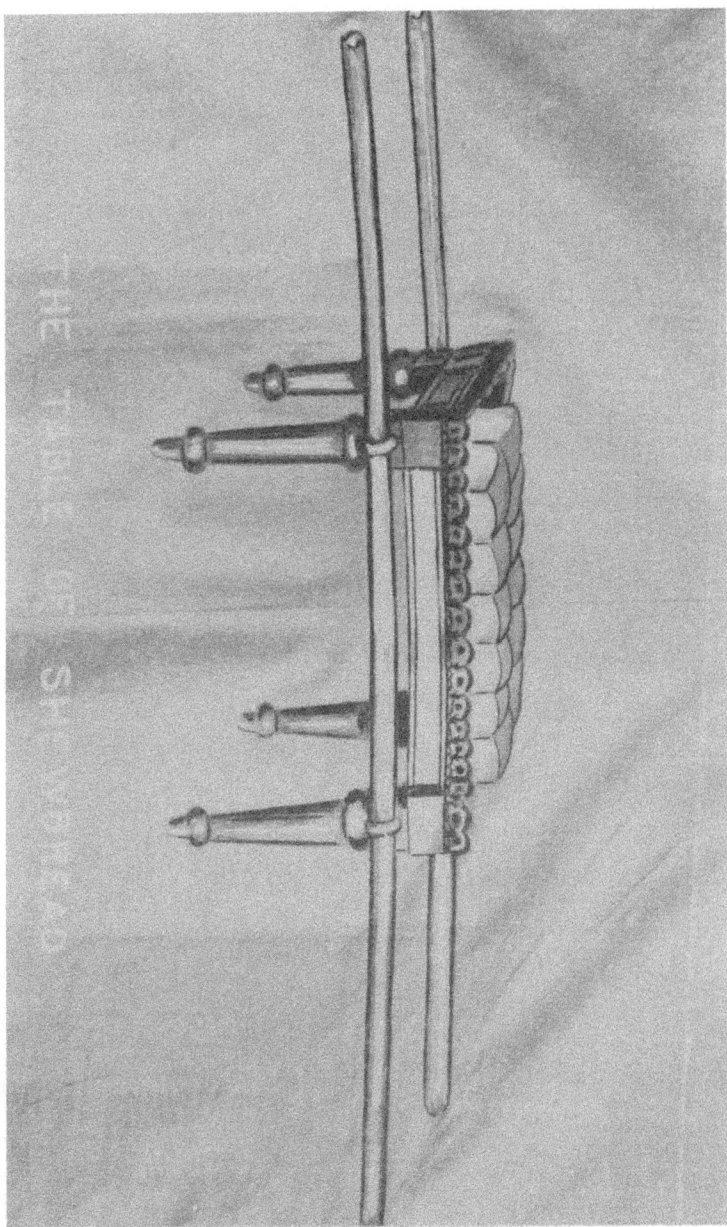

THE TABLE OF SHEWBREAD

Dimensions.—3 feet 6 inches high ; 2 feet 7 inches long ; 1 foot 9 inches wide.

CHAPTER IV.

THE HOLY PLACE.

WE will now consider the boards, bars, shew-bread, and candlestick. We are going to have some lessons on WOOD which represents the NATURAL. The wood that these boards and bars are made of is Shittim wood, which is the same as Acacia wood. This is the only tree in the desert that could furnish wood to build the Tabernacle. A type of you and me, the only wood God has to make His tabernacle of! In its natural state it is a hard looking old tree; you would never think you could make anything of it. It raises thorns. When the thorns come out you think there is but one, but as it grows longer, thorns come out of thorns. You, in your natural state, will produce thorns, and any one who gets near enough to you will get pricked. It also raises beans. If there is dirt enough, a tree will come where the beans drop. If one drops on a rock, when the rain comes along there will be a sprout. When you are taken out of the natural, you will stop the bean business. You will be out of baked bean sociables forever.

This wood is put into shape—mark the twenty-fifth chapter of Exodus: "Make these boards of Shittim wood standing up." The dimensions are given, and every board is made just alike. The tenons and rings are all described before he covers the wood with GOLD. There is a formation that God makes of us before He puts Divinity into us. There are a great many people around who have no Divinity—say! they are not built right. There are no NAKED Boards that do not get covered with Divinity. After the wood was put into Divine shape, it was covered all over with GOLD. You might be afraid that under the gold there would be some rotten wood; but there was not; it was dead, but not rotten; and when you are dead, you will never sprout again. I find people who profess sanctification who keep on sprouting; they are not *covered with gold.*

After this we find, in the thirtieth chapter, that there are two small pieces of silver, and each one had a socket in it. They were made out of the Atonement money of the Israelites, which was twenty-seven and a half cents apiece, taken alike from the rich and the poor. The rich must not give more, nor the poor less. These boards stood upon this silver foundation representing Atonement, and not only on it but IN it. For you will find the two tenons of the board fitting into the two sockets of the silver foundation so that every one of these

boards, spiritually speaking, stands not only on
the Atonement, but in the Atonement. And when
they paid this Atonement money the Scripture said
they should have no plague among them. The
trouble is at the BOTTOM of things. You had better
look down at your feet and see where you are
standing. A great many people have great trouble
with the Atonement. The Scripture says these
boards were set in order, and every board was just
alike, and no matter where they were put they
FITTED. There is such a thing as conformity without formality. If God can put you into shape, and
put Divinity into you, you will FIT! People who
fluctuate are not covered with gold. This shrink-
ing and swelling experience you will get rid of
when you are covered with gold. Some people do
not get the Divinity in them and on them, and
when a little rainstorm comes they are all swelled
up and they do not fit. You know you fit better
when you SHRINK than when you SWELL! I love
the saying of an old sea captain: "If you *let* God,
He will spiritualize every part of your life, and you
will be a spiritual man." Every one of the boards
has four rings on the side, and there are four bars
which go through these rings to hold the boards
together in the place He wants you to be. You
can not stand alone. I always pity people who say
they can get along without anybody—I can not do

it. I am the most independent-dependent man I
know of. It makes no difference where you are,
you will stand up straight and alongside the next
one. Put these little bars in, and everybody will
see that you have a fastening of human and Divine
that the devil can not do anything with. We must
have rings upon us for these bars to go through,
for this is not only an excursion when the evan-
gelists are around. Praise the Lord! But there
is a fifth bar, which goes from end to end, and is
"shot through." It was put right through the cen-
ter of the boards—right through our hearts—so
that we are held tight together! Outwardly this
tabernacle was not strong, but there was a fastening
inside that nobody could see. It comes through the
heart, and is not only human, but is also Divine.
Now, if you get into the tabernacle where God
wants you, you will have no trouble about backsliding. Besides all these Bars there are the Coverings, and the pressure is INWARD, not outward!
He holds you right where you are. You have the
desire to be with Christ; the pressure was that way
all the time. Stand up straight that God can be
glorified. Every one of these boards looked alike;
so do all the saints. All you can see is gold, gold,
gold. You need not take your knife either and
try to find black wood; you just keep still and not
cut through the Divinity. I like to look at the

saints. I am thinking now of dear Brother Pennington. He is a little higher than I am, but I look just like him. There is neither male nor female with God—this is strong kind of doctrine. It do n't feel very good to go through the plane and buzz-saw, but you will fit when He gets through with you. At the corners there were two boards joined together, and God can make corners of us. Some of us never had much corner on the stock market, but thank God we can have a corner on Divinity, for God wants to put two of us together and make a corner of us where we can get hold of victory. Do n't forget these boards stand on the Atonement money, and we must always stand upon the Atonement, too. I am so tired, for these days so many people leave the Atonement out. Some people came to our city and said there was no need of the Blood, no need of the Bible. This devilish stuff from the pit is being circulated here and there, and if you are not straightened by the bars through the rings and the heart, you will fall off in some of these places. If it had not been for the brethren, God only knows where I would have been standing to-day.

We will now consider the shewbread table for the "facebread." It is made of WOOD and covered with GOLD, and has two CROWNS. These crowns are Crowns of Glory. Many people spread a table,

but they do not put on it the bread God wants
there, so it is not crowned with Glory. This crown
holds the bread on. There is a crown underneath
to praise God for. Glory underneath, that crowns
our daily walk! There were rings too, and they
were in the LEGS. Some people need rings of eternal
endurance in the legs—they are *weak-kneed*. It
was PORTABLE, and God wants you and me to *carry*
the bread that He means us to have. It is a "Com-
mandment" concerning this bread, and God tells
us just what kind of Flour to bring and how it is
to be baked, and then it is to be left before the Lord.
When you hear of a new doctrine that claims to
be bread, like Christian Science, you let it stay
before the Lord "six days" and see whether it *is*
bread or not. Some of you would get rid of this
spiritual dyspepsia if you would do this. This
bread is a sweet type—it is UNLEAVENED bread.
In the Scripture, leaven is a type of sin, and the
sure work of sin, no other type just like it. You
go and mix up a batch of bread, and if you do n't
bake it pretty quickly, it will drive you out of
doors. There is more devil in bread than in whisky.
You put a little saleratus in and put it in the oven
or it may poison the whole family. That table was
to hold up bread and keep it in the presence of
God until He put endorsement on it; then it was
to be eaten in the Holy Place. If people only ate

in THE HOLY PLACE there would be less backsliding.

Let us now turn to the candlestick. We now pass from individual to CHURCH relations. We have been talking about different members, now we are getting to organization. When God speaks of the candlestick, He uses the pronoun "His," and while the standing shaft represents Christ (and nobody can have Christian standing except as they stand in Him), yet out from it goes those six branches. The middle shaft has one more bowl and one more flower than these side ones! You don't want to say, "Do not look at me; look at Christ." If you do not reflect Christ so that an old drunkard can take you as a type of Christ, it is about time we stopped showing false light. Paul says we are a savor of life unto life" (2 Cor. ii, 16). I know what I am talking about, dear ones. I knew nothing about the Bible, but I saw a pure person once, and put my feet in their steps, and before long I was on the road to Glory. This candlestick is of pure gold and has seven branches; it has a standing place over against the shewbread. It is of PURE GOLD—that is *Divine;* and you can not manufacture a human organization out of it. God Almighty organized the Church; man's hand had nothing to do with it. It is a place of victory and of glory. I pity a minister who has to humanly organize and run a Church. Each

branch of the candlestick stands on a pomegranate,
and the lamps are filled with olive oil. The command was to bring "pure olive oil beaten out."
The olive tree has some lessons. It brings forth
fruit gradually. The first thing you see is a white
blossom. It has a white blossom cover around it,
and when the wind blows against that tree, the
world around it is made white. When you are in
blossom and the winds blow around you, things
ought to be covered with whiteness and fragrance.
That is the *first* experience, and when people look
at you they will never think of any olives, but
they are there. *They* are the second experience,
and bring forth the precious oil. With this pure
olive oil, *beaten out,* the lamps were to be "caused"
to burn, and to burn always and continually before
the Lord. There were seven lights in this candlestick. This signifies a perfect light; and while they
were burning the officiating priest comes along with
snuffers and snuff-dishes (of pure gold!). He
does not seem to use the same snuffers and snuff-
dishes for each one, but they are all "his" snuffers
and snuff-dishes. These lamps must sit on the
pure-gold candlestick—if you sit anywhere else, you
will backslide in twenty-four hours; the Scripture
shows this plainly. I met a minister last week in
my old home-place, and he said, "Charles, how do
you do?" I said, "I am on the top shelf, and I feel

THE BOARDS AND BARS.

like jumping over the stove-pipe." He commenced to wiggle, and I said, "God wants you to be at your best, with a clean heart;" and he said, "I ought to have it; I never was so tired in my life." He was not on the pure candlestick. The High Priest tends to these lamps. You just sit on the pure candlestick, and it makes no difference where He puts you, there are seven branches, and He will set you afire and you will have no more trouble with the "baptism of fire." He will come along morning and evening and trim and fill you, and you stay there and get filled. I have nothing at stake, and if He don't fill me it's His fault, not mine. He fills you up at three o'clock, and although this and that goes against you, I want to tell you, you must burn over night. But glory to God there will be a morning, and He will then come around. He fills you in the evening, and in the morning He will trim you, and He will bring His GOLDEN snuff-dish and snuffers, and He will snuff you when you have burned through the night, and He will put the ashes away where no one will know anything about them. He will let no newspaper print it and no stenographer put it down! Glory to God! I have seen it so many times, you have been burning through the night and no one but God knows what you are going through. Some one might say, "I do not seem to have so much light as when I was

first sanctified." But if you are where He wants
you, He will come along and trim you. You have
seen somebody, and you knew they were going
through trouble, and praise the Lord, I do love it
so much, that this very smut was blessed in the
sight of Jesus, and he did not allow any uncircum-
cised hands to touch it. He takes the smut and
casts it out where there are no backsliders or such
things. HE CARRIES IT OFF. "Brother So-and-So
has been burning through the night and has had a
hard experience and I will fix him up and take away
the trimmings, and nobody will know where they
are put." You can see that you must stay on the
pure candlestick, or when He comes to trim and fill
the lamp you won't be there! "Well, I don't seem
to be as full as I was." Look at your feet and see
where you are standing. Well, well, well! He
don't come around THERE to fill. You will backslide in twenty-four hours! Are you giving an im-
perfect light? If so, something is lacking in the
perfect light, for it took the *whole seven lamps* to
make the perfect light. There would have been
no light in this place if the candlestick had not
shined! There were no extinguishers to these lamps
and we must not let the devil put any on.

THE ALTAR OF INCENSE

Dimensions.—1 foot 2 inches square; 3 feet 6 inches high.

CHAPTER V.

ALTAR OF INCENSE (OR HOLY ALTAR) AND COVERINGS.

WE will now finish the subject of the Holy Place, bringing out the golden altar, the type of prayer. How much we need to know how to pray! The way to know how to pray is to PRAY. The only way in which you can keep yourself in the love of God is to pray in the Holy Ghost. In prayer of this kind it is not the individual who prays, but He makes intercession for you according to the will of God.

The thirtieth chapter of Exodus, which describes the golden altar, is one of the greatest chapters in the whole Bible. This golden altar is close to the veil, and it is the highest piece of furniture connected with the whole Tabernacle service. God said it should be made of shittim wood, and that horns should be put on it (symbolic of power), and after the horns were put on He covers it with gold and surmounts it with a crown. Beautiful type of prayer! You can not pray until you have the Divine righteousness of the Holy Ghost. How much talk there is with the tongue to please somebody's ears. But real prayer is talking with God. Billy Bray is said once to have picked up his hat, and there was a hole in it, and he said, "Father, I want a new hat. Do n't you see the hole in this one?" That was real prayer. That was being in Divine righteousness. People say, "O you pray for me." God wants YOU where you can ask for anything you need, and receive it.

Then there were to be staves for it. It was to be portable! Praise God! anywhere you go, if you have a golden altar with you, you can pray and ask and be answered! It is a perfect treat to pray all night, a perfect treat to be with Him and talk of this old lost world. The altar was four square. You can pray on all four sides of it, and there is a place between the altar and the veil. And taking the veil to represent the flesh, I like to get in between the veil and the altar and say, "Lord, save my old body!"

As to the incense, we do not know very much about the ingredients. Onycha was a shell-fish that had eyes, lungs, and stomach. You know how these shell-fish just shut themselves up and let their enemies bite the top of the shell. The devil will just pester you, but shut yourself in your shell. I remember one time a woman fell and broke her collar-bone, and she was seventy-nine years old. I went to see her and began to pray, and all that the old devil would let me think of was, "Seventy-nine, seventy-nine, seventy-nine, and all her bones are chalk." But shut yourself in your shell where the old shark of unbelief can not bite you.

No one of the ingredients of the incense had a perfume of itself. Prayer only smells good when it comes in contact with fire. Then how beautiful it is! Onycha of itself was most disagreeable; but when it was mixed with the three others it was all right. Galbanum and frankincense were types of Jesus. He says this perfume was to be a confection compounded together, just as much of one as of another. We are to mix the sweetmeats at the golden altar. This is holy confectionery. We are not to make anything else that smells like it; there must be no imitation. False prayer will cut you off from the house of Israel. Let the Holy Ghost do the praying. Sometimes He will cause you to pray when everybody will pray with you, and sometimes He will pray through you when everybody is sleeping.

In the Book of Revelation it speaks of the golden vials and of the incense beaten small, and after it was offered the Lion of Judah prevailed and opened the Book. O, this incense (prayer) that is *beaten small!* The saints may be dead, but their prayers are *bottled up.* In that wonderful scene in heaven which we have just alluded to, it says that another angel came and offered much incense, with the prayers of the saints (the margin says added to the prayers of the saints), and it goes up, and there follows a half-hour of stillness and the answer came down. I ran away to escape from my Father's prayers; but he prayed till there was a stillness in heaven. His prayers were beaten small, and God heard them. A minister once preached, and was surprised that after his sermon souls sought the Lord for His pardoning grace. He told some one he could not understand why that sermon should have taken such effect; but upon going to the place of his entertainment he was met by an old lame woman, a saint of God, who greeted him with these words: "Did they come? Did they come?" *She* had prayed, and *beaten it small,* and God had answered. A woman once had a daughter who wandered away to the city and lived in sin; but the mother followed her with her prayers. After a long time the girl's heart was touched, and she said, "I will go home and see if mother will forgive me." She approached the house at night; but a lamp was burning. She tried the door; it was left unlatched. She opened the door, and a voice said, "Ellen, is that YOU?" I get broken to pieces when I dwell upon this subject. O, let us learn to *beat it small!*

We will now consider the coverings. The first was fine linen, and fine linen means FINE linen, and

represents Divine righteousness. We can not get such linen now as this was. I know of only one piece in the world, and that is in the British Museum, and in that piece there are five hundred and forty threads to the warp, and one hundred and ten to the woof, per inch. This arrangement is contrary to that of Yankee manufacture. Thank God that it is! When God grafts a tree He grafts it contrary to nature. It is the same with the fine linen. Another term for this linen is *twisted* linen, and the Lord twists us until that which is natural is twisted into line with Him and His plans.

The colors worked upon this fine linen were blue, purple, and scarlet. Forty-two times in the Book of Exodus that order is given. The Divine Embroiderer worked His "cunning" work into the fine linen. The first color He works into you and me is BLUE—blue from heaven. After a rain the heavens look black; but if the sun shone the sky would look blue; so with the sea. If you never had light you would not have the BLUE sea. Blue with light means heaven. It is the bright shining of the light that brings out the blue.

Then the purple; that is a royal color. There is a kingly character about it, and it is put into our life *here* when we are anointed kings and priests of the Lord. Also it brings out the type of our coming King. Scarlet brings out the suffering.

4

And when these purer colors of blue and scarlet are brought together you get purple! Take the fellowship of His sufferings and the blue of heaven, and it brings out the royal purple. There are so few that like to be brought to His death. They will go along on the excursions and baked-bean sociables and that line; but when it comes to suffering and doing as He did! Suppose we have to go barefoot and have blood running from out our mouths; we have heaven enough later on!

After this the Divine Embroiderer put in the cherubi.n of gold. Now take the blue and scarlet and put yellow to it, and you will get WHITE. Add some of the gold of Divinity, and you are perfectly white! These angels represent redeemed beings. They are not the kind that never knew anything about salvation.

On the edge of each one of these pieces in the covering He put in fifty loops of blue on a side, and thus one selvidge is joined to another. A selvidge is a finish. Some people never had any selvidge. There are lots of "raw-edge" Christians! These loops are attached together with gold. We may be one tabernacle in unity, glory to God! It is not a couple of loops on a side, but FIFTY. And so these strips are put together, and it makes a glorious covering. And all of this God does in our lives; the Scripture is so plain. The white linen is the righteousness of the saints, and upon this foundation the Great Embroiderer does the work; and this work was "cunning" work. How expressive that word cunning is!

The next covering was of goat's hair. This was put together with brass taches and one extra breadth, which hung over the front of the Tabernacle. Any one coming through the gate would see the goat's hair covering spun by the wise-hearted (not wise-headed!) women. This hair was taken from the goats set apart for the Lord, and the thought of Christ bearing our sins as the Great Scapegoat is here brought out.

The next covering was ram's skin dyed red. To this there are no dimensions whatever. I praise the Lord that there were no dimensions, for that means that it is big enough for every possible need. Had there been any dimensions it might have left Charles Potter out! Its being dyed RED expresses consecration. The ram must be slain, and not only slain, but skinned. It is awful to think of giving up your life, of being flayed for the Lord; yet some dear ones have had to do it. And Jesus went farther than that to bring you and me to God.

The next covering is a badger skin. That is the outside covering. It may have been made of the Mediterranean seal or of the badger brought from Persia. A badger is a little animal; but it is a great digger. Praise the Lord for Christians that have digging qualities! Some Christians have no claws, and they can neither *hold on* nor dig. It is a hard animal to kill. The old natives used to subject this animal to test after test; but he lived through them all. His hair was said to go through his skin and take hold of the very flesh. It was splendid protection from the rain. These qualities were brought out in the life of Jesus, our Divine Protector. Remember, this badger skin was the outside covering. A great many people get no further than this badger skin. They say they believe in the *sufferings of Christ;* but if you go no further than the badger's skin you would smother there. A great many people like to be going around "doing good." But first the Holy Ghost must do some work *in you,* and the embroidery is the same on both sides. Generally you put embroidery work on one side, the side for folks to look at; but holy work is on both sides, and both sides are the same. Everything you advertise is *in the store.* I went into a store the other day to buy something I saw in the window; but they gave me something different. When I asked for the same thing that was in the window, I found they had no duplicates on the inside! When the Tabernacle was journeying these coverings were used to cover the ark and the shewbread and the golden altar.

THE ALTAR OF BURNT OFFERING.

Dimensions.—7 feet 6 inches square; 4 feet 6 inches high.

CHAPTER VI.

THE OUTER COURT.

THE outer court was lit by natural light, sunlight. Its dimensions were to be an hundred cubits (one hundred and fifty feet) in length, and fifty cubits (seventy-five feet) in breadth, *everywhere*. Thank God for an experience that will measure the same under any and all circumstances, in the shop and in the kitchen! Around this court were sixty pillars, made of acacia wood covered with brass, and having a brass foundation. These pillars are all alike in size and material, and are placed equi-distant. A pillar has the spiritual signification of *truth*. The brass foundation signifies *judgment*. This court of truth and judgment is the Great Tribunal that judges the world. Any doctrine, assuming to be *true,* that does not *judge the world* is defective.

The pillars had hooks and fillets of silver, and were supported by cords and brass nails. The top chapter of the pillar was also made of silver, which stands for atonement. Upon this frame-work of atonement, truth, and judgment was hung the fine linen curtain representing the righteousness of the

saints. May God make our Churches such pillars
of truth that the linen shall not drag in the dirt!
Surely pillars of *truth* are the only supports that the
linen of *righteousness* can be hung upon. This linen
is so fine it can be seen through. It is no secret
order; it is the transparent righteousness of the
saints. But though it can be seen through, it could
not be touched by profane hands. The only way to
enter the court was by the gate.

Having entered we first come to the brazen
altar. This altar was made of the brass from the
censers of the men who perished in the rebellion of
Korah. It was *portable*. When an animal from the
herd or flock or a fowl was to be offered, its head
was first to be removed; then it was to be flayed
and cut in pieces (the skin belonged to the officiating priest), and its fat and head were first put upon
the altar. Its inwards were then washed (typical
of our affections), and its legs (typical of our
walk); the unclean parts were cast away, and the
rest was burned upon the altar. How *we* need first
to get rid of our *heads!* How many people find
their heads in the way of their hearts! The one
making sacrifice puts his hand upon the head of the
victim, thus becoming identical with it and making
it his substitute. This offering takes place in the
evening, and burns until morning. *This* fire never
goes out; it is kept alive by the wood offering.

The wood offering is furnished at the time of sacrifice. It was laid upon Isaac as he went up Mt. Moriah. At Bethshemesh it was the new Philistine cart. For Gideon it was his father's idolatrous grove. Elisha's was the plowing instruments of the oxen, which he left in the field. While the sacrifice is being consumed the officiating priest stood by with a flesh hook. He looked out all through the dark night. With this hook (not a pitchfork!) he pulled the offering towards him, and he saw that no part was left unconsumed. Have you ever *felt* the flesh hook while you were upon the altar? The work *must be* THOROUGH. And the priest constantly tastes the shoulder (strength) of the offering as it roasts, and it pleases him to find it properly done; and the Lord tenderly watches us when we offer to Him, and the taste pleases Him of a thoroughly made sacrifice, and it is a sweet savor unto the Lord as He smells the smoke from our complete offering, and He feeds upon us and is thoroughly satisfied. Glory to God! In performing this service the priest has on linen garments, and when the sacrifice is burned one hundred and fifty pounds may be reduced to about a pint of ashes! The trouble with some is that they do not burn *all night*. There is no other light in the court that night. The light of that sacrifice (smoldering on when no one stands by but the priest) is there alone; no electric-lights,

no appreciative illumination; nothing but the fire
that does its solemn work. The white ties and
broadcloth are burned! Nothing is left but ashes.
These are put in a copper pan with a copper shovel,
and placed upon the east side of the Tabernacle.
The priest then changes his clothes, and when the
new light comes and the morning breaks these ashes
are taken away and put in a clean place—the place
of ashes. And the Lord giveth "beauty for ashes."
Ashes do not revolve around the comforts of home
life; do not need to stay by "Martha," but will go
to the foreign field. O, thank God! there comes
a time when we really get to be ashes! Then the
altar has done its work and we are taken off. So
many are always on; but there is a time when the
work is complete, and new light comes, and we are
put in a *clean place* outside the camp. We do not
know geographically where this clean place was;
but it was on the east side, where the first light was.
Spiritually it is where He is. Let us go unto Him,
bearing His reproach! Here we can offer a new
offering, even praise to God continually. Every
truly sanctified soul is with Him, and like Him, and
outside the camp. Covered by the officiating priest
in a clean place, there is no more struggling; nothing but *cleanness*. Glory to God!

Next we come to the laver. It was made from
the mirrors of the women. They surrendered their

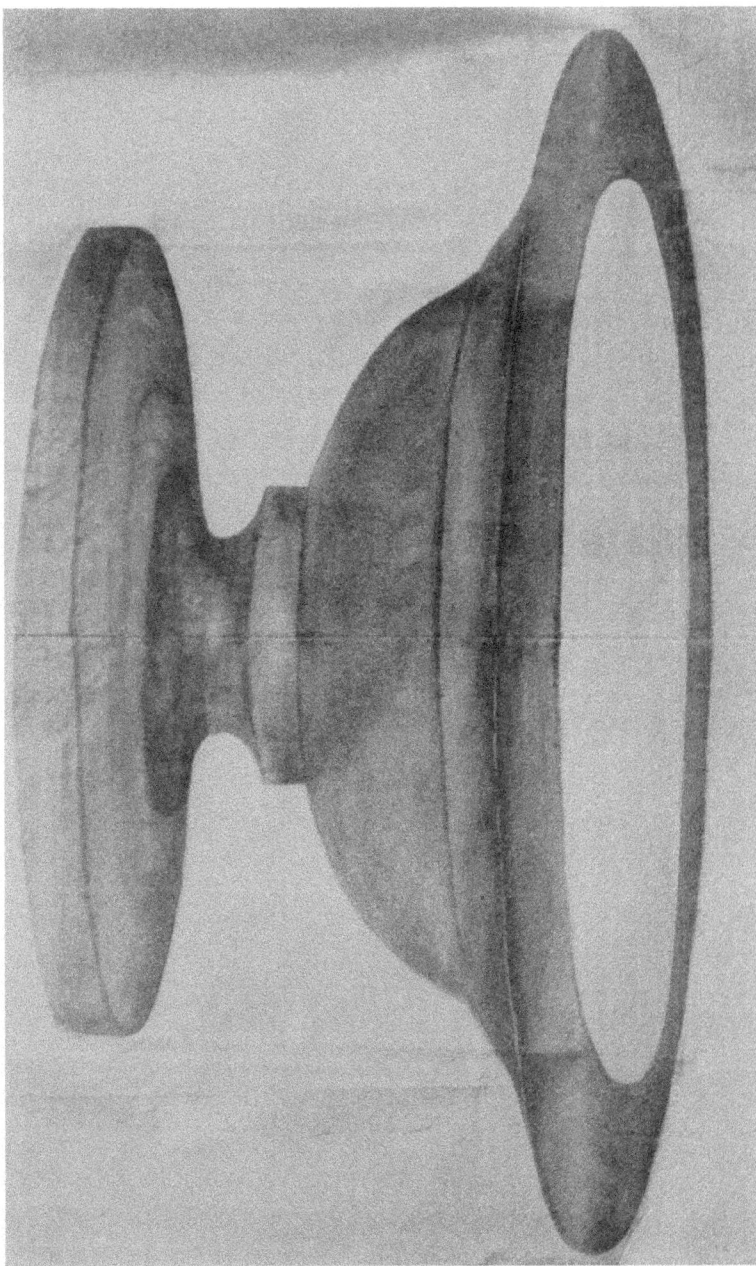

The Brazen Laver.

looking-glasses, and looked into the Word of God! God's Word is the laver and the looking-glass. This laver stood between the brazen altar and the door of service. First came the *gate,* then the *altar,* then the *laver,* then *service.* It is to wash away our defilement as we go through this sinful world. We look into its polished copper. How it does show our defilement! Then we wash the stains away in the water it contains. The Apostle James talks about a man who looks and forgets; but that is "vain." We *ought* to look and then wash, that we die not. So many have died because they failed to wash. Wherewithal shall a young man cleanse his way? By taking heed thereto according to Thy Word. I have cleansed my hands in innocency. So shall we compass thine altars, O Lord! When Jesus, with a basin and girded with a towel, washed the disciples' feet, the thought is that He gave them a laver bath. This is also the thought in the passage, Christ loved the Church, washing it with laver bath, that He might have a spotless Church. The washing of water through the Word, "Now are ye clean through the Word that I have spoken unto you." Around this laver was sprinkled the blood; and from His wounded side there came forth blood and water.

We shall finally be judged by the Word of God. It is now our laver, and we ought to be lavers for other people to look in and see by our lives their faults.   Did you ever notice a sparrow take its morning bath?   Notice how it puts its *head* under first!   When you next stand in front of your wash-stand, ask yourself whether you have, spiritually speaking, taken your "morning dip."

CHAPTER VII.

THE RED HEIFER AND THE RIBBON OF BLUE.

(Numbers xix, and xv, 27-41.)

THE Book of Numbers is a spiritual guide-book, a "path-finder" for the soul! The lesson of the red heifer is the lesson of substitution. The heifer is a female, red (typical of the blood of Christ), without spot or blemish, and upon which a yoke had never come. The female gender here used brings out the tenderness, "the motherhood" of Jesus. With what tenderness He seems to mother the poor lost drunkard!

This red heifer was brought to Eleazer. Eleazer means God's help. Lord, increase the Eleazers! The heifer, being slain before his face, its blood was to be sprinkled before the Tabernacle seven times, and then she was to be burned in his sight. Her skin, and her flesh, and her blood, with her dung, shall he burn, and while burning the priest shall cast into the midst cedar-wood, hyssop, and scarlet. One that is clean now gathers up the ashes, and, putting them in water, forms the "water of separation."

David surely was thinking of this water of separation, when, after slaying Uriah, he said, "Purge
me with hyssop, and I shall be clean." When we
seek the Lord we should confess the worst there is;
we should admit that we have touched a dead body
"slain in the open field." Do not whistle past the
graveyard. Confess the worst, then say, "Purge me
with hyssop." The sprinkling of this water sepa-
rates us from the heathen and from all dead bodies.
(See Ezek. xxxvi, 24, 25.)

In considering the sin of ignorance (Num. xv,
27-29), let us note that it is hard to commit it when
we watch over each other. Yes, you are your
brother's keeper; in one sense as much as you are
your own. Many times the PEOPLE need to go forward for prayers more than the one who falls. The
responsibility rests not upon the pastor only, but upon
the whole flock. Once when I had a felon upon my
finger my whole body worked hard to benefit the
sick member until the difficulty was largely overcome. A sin of ignorance is "before the Lord."
This implies that one must have a spiritual standing in the sight of the Lord to commit one.

For presumptuous sin there is no forgiveness.
(Num. xv, 30-37.) "There is a sin UNTO DEATH."
"There remaineth no more sacrifice for sin." No
FORGIVENESS in this world or the world to come.
The unpardonable sin is to sin against the Holy

Ghost. God is anxious that you and I should not commit sin.

We will now turn to the ribbon of blue. (Num. xv, 37-41.) Notice that it is on the SKIRTS of the garment (not in the button-hole!); suggestive of the daily walk. It was on *all sides* of the garment; not just on the front to be seen on Sundays! It was BLUE, the color of heaven. A man do n't go according to his own heart. When you *step* the blue ribbon shows, and folks would see it if you went to the theater! Do n't make it too WIDE. And do n't make it too NARROW. It should be the width of a rib-band. WITH it you are safe anywhere. Jesus wore it, and when the sick woman touched the hem of His garment she was made every whit whole. Praise the Lord!

CHAPTER VIII.

CONSECRATION OF THE LEVITES.

We will now turn to the consecration of the Levites. A Levite means one that is *joined*. They that are joined to the Lord are one spirit. The tribe of Levi was really the thirteenth tribe, though it was not thus spoken of in the Bible. Levi was the third son of Leah, and was in his mother a type of the law. This tribe redeemed its unsavory reputation (and was accepted by the Lord, instead of the first born) after the golden calf was made, and Moses cried, "Who is on the Lord's side?" and Levi volunteered to cut loose from everything and be true to God. It was a complete consecration.

In the chapter that tells about the consecration of the Levites (Num. viii, 5-23), the golden candlestick is mentioned. The seven lamps of it were lighted as the Lord commanded, and they having been lit, these Levites, candidates for God's service, were to be sprinkled with the "waters of separation." Some people say they are living in all the light they have, and others are praying for more light; but if they walk by the light of the Word they would have plenty of light. Where are you *living*—near

THE HIGH PRIEST ON THE DAY OF ATONEMENT.

the candlestick, or in a cellar where the light does not come?

After being sprinkled with the "water of separation" they were to shave themselves. This meant they were to cut the natural growth off their flesh. The great trouble with ministers of the gospel is, that they have so much natural growth that they do not get the supernatural things.

Next the Levite was to wash his clothes (this signifies the coverings and the habits), and so make himself clean. God expects you and me to have clean habits. There is nothing said here about what kind of clothing they wore; but I do not know what God would say about the rigs of some of his Levites now! After their clothes were cleaned they were to assemble before the Tabernacle, where they were to be examined before the Lord. A meat offering of fine flour was made with a young bullock; and another young bullock was taken for a sin offering, and the Levite, by putting his hand on the head of this bullock, made the offering identical with himself, and acknowledged the consecration. O, it means so much to acknowledge the consecration! One is made just as clean as the cleansing power of the blood that is applied. We are made as clean as the blood of Christ. Marvelous thought! The blood of Jesus Christ His Son cleanseth us from all sin.

Now Moses offers the consecrated Levite to the Lord, and the Levite acknowledges it; and from that time that man and his family go into the service of the Lord. There was no entrance requirement of etiquette or education. He was not required to have hair parted in the middle or to gesticulate properly! *After the consecration* he is ready for the ministry. He entered service at twenty-five years of age, and remained there until fifty years of age. The juniors bore the burdens, and the elders waited upon the Lord and enjoyed the fellowship of the brethren.

Among the Levites were three chief families; the Gershonites, who were the oldest and had charge of the curtains and hangings (to them were given two wagons and four oxen); the Merarites, who had charge of the boards and sockets (and they had four wagons and eight oxen); the Kohathites, who, because Aaron belonged to this tribe, had charge of the sacred vessels. These Levites pitched immediately around the Tabernacle. No plagues nor any disease came into their midst. They believed in Divine healing! They had no land nor any bank account; the Lord was their inheritance. They had charge of the cities of refuge, whither the man slayer might flee and be safe. Praise God for a place of refuge! They commanded no salary, but had a part of what the people gave, a tenth. There was also the festive tithe for the meeting, and the alms tithe for the poor. When this was paid the offerers could *command* God's blessing upon themselves. God promises that he will pour out such a blessing that we shall not be able to contain it. He says He will open the windows of heaven to do this! We read in the Scripture of a man named Joses who was a Levite, and as such he had no business to possess any land, and when the Holy Ghost got hold of him he sold all that he had and laid it at the apostle's feet, and had his name changed from Joses to Barnabas (son of consolation). If we do with our means as God says, we will be sons of consolation. So many people weigh one hundred and eighty pounds in the natural, who do not weigh two ounces in the spiritual. God, deliver us from scant-weight sanctified Christians! If we are wholly consecrated, we can ask God to "rebuke the devourer" for our sake. When he is after our children, we can say "Lord, rebuke the devil for my sake." But in order to get this blessing, we must give God His part; we must pay the full price.

CHAPTER IX.

THE HOLY ANOINTING OIL.
(Ex. xxx.)

GOD has a kingdom of priests. All are priests who belong to the kingdom; but we must obey the Covenant. This is a wonderful thought! All we must do is to have ears open to hear His voice, and be obedient to the Covenant. The thirtieth chapter of Exodus commences with the golden altar; then follows the atonement money, the brazen laver, and the anointing oil. *Notice this order;* and notice how it says, *"Take thou* ALSO. I like that word "also." Some people do n't have any *also* about them; but you must also take the OIL when you are sanctified!

We are then told what the oil is made of. One part is pure myrrh. Myrrh is typical of liberty, pure liberty. Many people have a liberty that is not PURE liberty. There are five hundred shekels of pure liberty! This oil is made of five different parts, and God is particular just how much of each part there shall be. Myrrh is the first one named, and the liberty which it typifies is not the kind that comes *after death;* do not go over the horns of the moon; but stay *here* a little while, and have *pure liberty.*

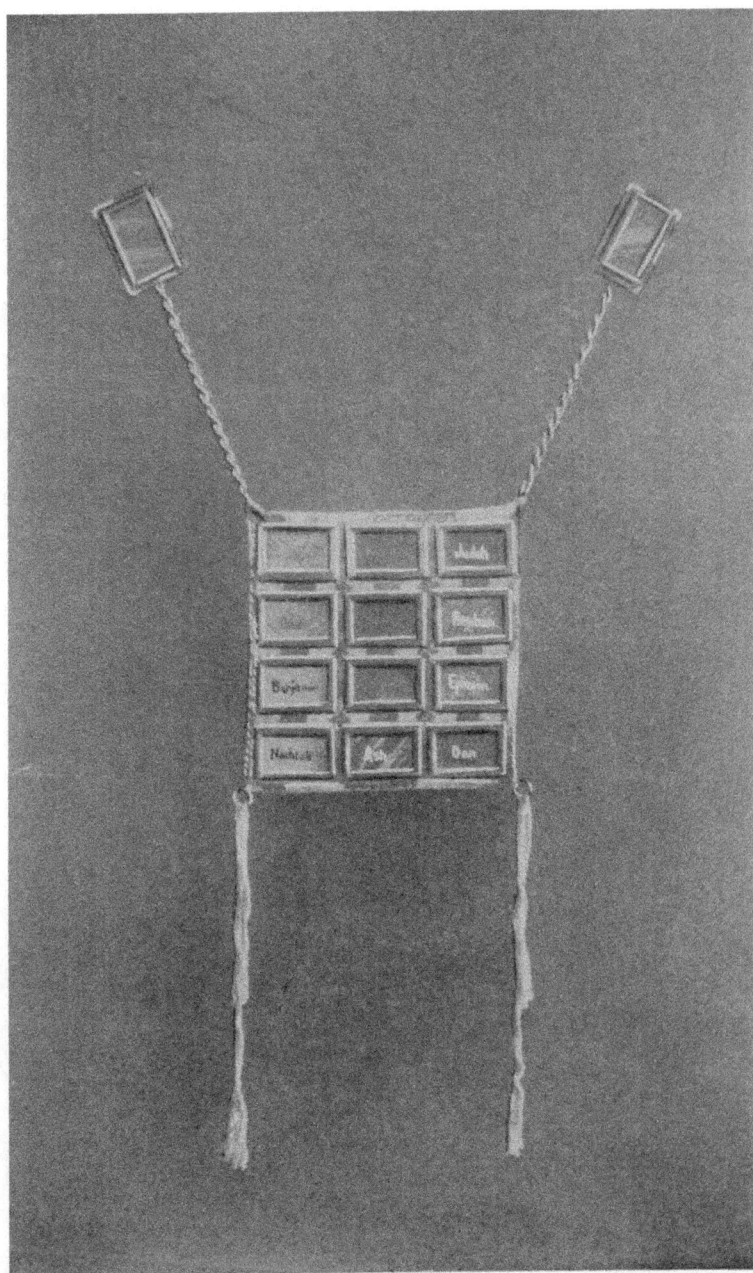

THE BREASTPLATE.

The next spice is sweet cinnamon. We are all familiar with it. Of this there are to be 250 shekels, one-half as much as of the myrrh. It is the bark of a tree; it is a stimulant medicine. My mother used to give it to me when I was young, and sometimes when it was old it was bitter; but in the young tree it is sweet. Some people seem to have an anointing oil; but the cinnamon in it is bitter!

The next is calamus. There are 250 shekels of sweet calamus. It is like canes of sweet flag, and grows by the running water; the water of the Word! It stands for discernment. Some people, if they have their hair parted in the middle, think they are all right. It takes discernment (calamus) to tell them! SWEET *calamus* (judgment and discernment), that comes from the Word of God! You must have a wisdom that will go beneath nice etiquette if you are to be a successful worker for God.

Cassia is the next. The word cassia means to stoop; it brings out the thought of humility. He puts in *500 shekels of this*. Some people think that when they get the anointing oil they can do as they please; but He puts in 500 shekels of humility! If you have an entire sanctification that makes you do as you have a mind to, that is the devil without sanctification. The man that is sanctified is the most humble man on earth. The most humble person the world ever saw was a man who never knew any sin. Cassia is humility, and is *the same in quantity as the myrrh liberty!*

The last element is the olive oil. There is a whole measure of it. The olive has two cells and two seeds, except when it is deformed or abortion is practiced. Spiritually there is a great deal of deformity and abortion, because people have only one cell instead of two. Notice anybody that does not believe in the second blessing! God has loaded up even the little plant to teach us the lesson! By means of this olive oil all the spices are compounded together, and make the WHOLE ointment—five in one. Some say, "I am humble; but I have no liberty." You pray to be sanctified wholly, and you will get ALL the qualities of the oil! It is compounded together, and you can not pick out just the part you would like to have, and leave the rest. Be sanctified, and you will have liberty. With this precious ointment the Tabernacle (and its furniture and its vessels) was to be anointed. It is about time the *furniture* we worship God with was anointed.

There was to be no ointment made like it. Any one who compounded any was to be cut off from the house of Israel. The most natural supernatural person is a sanctified person. The oil must not be put upon strangers nor upon man's flesh. These things will cut you off from the house of Israel. Oil *follows* blood all the way through the Scriptures. The oil only goes where the blood is. The oil is a type of unity; not "the Fatherhood of God and fellowship of man," but the unity of a holy family whose members are born from above. My name is Potter, but I am a son of God born from above.

You must be anointed in time of MOURNING. When it touches you, you are full of gladness. Get rid of your mourning, and get the oil of glory! Everything that is good belongs to the anointed ones. The peaches and pears that are first ripe belong to you; you are the firstborn. The devil wants to give us a lot of old rotten fruit; but I do n't want it. We must not defile the anointing. The one that had that sacred oil poured on his head must not come in contact with death or any dead bodies— not only dead bodies, but dead folks! You can not defile yourself for your father or mother. A great many people, when their father and mother will not go their way, go with them, and they defile their anointing. *You* stay in the sanctuary, no matter where they go.

When this oil is poured upon your head it will take out the wrinkles. When you get sanctified out go the wrinkles! Some people have a spooky kind of a look. If they were ENTIRELY sanctified it would go away! There is a fullness of this oil. The Scripture says, *"Do not lack any of it."* All of these spices have an individual perfume. Myrrh will smell

for a year and a half if taken alone; but you pack
it down in oil and the perfume will last forever.
You get saturated with the baptism of the Holy
Ghost, and you will last forever.   You will never
backslide.   No matter what your surroundings, the
devil must keep his hands off.   Lord, help us right
here!   I knew a poor girl.   Her name was Delia.
She was in our house five weeks.   She went through
the same place where she had been in sin, and men
touched their hats to her.   When she was dead,
around her poor old body many were saved.   Since
I stopped drinking only three times have I been
invited to take a glass, and one of those times was
when I had been bargaining with a Jew who kept
a clothing store, and he said he would make a bar-
gain and we would have a drink on it; and I would
not have had that if it had not been for my old
dickering!   I saw a man to-day that I used to
gamble with; but it had no effect upon me!

People can smell this anointing oil.   You do not
have to force out the perfume; it will smell in spite
of you!   When you come in contact with holy men
and women, this oil will make your nostrils tingle,
and awe will come over you.   John says it is an
anointing that "abideth."   Dear ones do n't shrink
when God wants to put the anointing oil on you!
This oil never smells like *tobacco* or *beer!*   I heard
a minister once say that he was surely sanctified;

but one day he came on me quickly, and I saw him holding *behind him* a half stump. What did he hold it *behind* him for?

How much belongs to the anointing oil! Safety, victory, power. It will quicken your mortal body. Everybody can have it. I want to tell you God is not sanctified where there is uncleanness, no matter where; not while soap and water is as cheap as now. God will call you to walk in some *new* places. You have never walked there before. And there are some places that you used to go that you can not go now. He gives you discernment to see where you can, and can not, go. You get sanctified, and your husband may say, "You do so and so;" but you can not do it. It makes things crosswise; but you can not defile your sanctification. If you do you will lose your crown. Lord, help us here! Look right back in your life, and see the steps that have brought darkness into your soul! You have defiled the ointment, you have lost the liberty, you have lost the discernment! He will restore you, so that you will know where you are. Lord, we thank You for all that this means to us! Help us never again, Lord, to defile the ointment! Help us never again to come in contact with dead people! They *were alive once,* and they *died.* May we walk in Thy presence, walk as He walked! We thank Thee for the ointment, for all its stimulant medicine, for all its humility, for the completeness of the whole! When anointed we can look into Thy face and Thou into our faces, and the crown of the Lord will be on our heads. We can look into Thy face because Thou art not ashamed to call us brethren. If an unsaved one or a backslider reads this, I beg of the Lord to touch them, that they may be saved and see what it is to be saved!

THE HIGH PRIEST IN OFFICIAL ROBES.

CHAPTER X.

THE HIGH PRIEST AND HOLY GARMENTS.

(Exodus xxviii and xxix. Leviticus viii and xvi.)

As we discuss the subject of the high priest, let us notice that besides the high priest there was the ordinary priest and the priestly or Levitical tribe. All priests were Levites, but all Levites were not priests. We will first consider the consecration of the high priest and his sons. They were to be brought unto the door of the tabernacle of the congregation, and Moses was there to wash them with water and to place upon them the holy garments, and then upon the head of the high priest was to be poured the anointing oil. Next, offerings were to be made; first a sin offering. A young bullock in the height of its strength is the highest type of a sin offering. Then, if the sin offering is complete, comes the ram of the burnt offering, and the ram of consecration. The rams are to be slain, and the different parts taken in minute consecration. When God undertakes to examine an offering, He looks upon the very inside. Thou shalt take the fat that is upon the entrails, and the caul that is above the liver, and the two kidneys and the fat of the kidneys, the inwards and the legs. This is not a subject that people like to talk about, or want to have brought out, but it needs to be brought out. The consecration of the priest should be your consecration and mine. Some people think they can consecrate everything in the old life to God, but God is not picking up every old thing no more than we are. People talk about consecrating their tobacco to God, but you can't do it, for He won't take it. With the blood of the ram of consecration, the priest's right ear and right thumb and great toe of the right foot were to be touched. I am so glad the foot was to be touched—it is so good to have a Holy Ghost walk, a walk touched by the blood of Jesus.

After the blood has touched them comes the waive offering, and a thing once waived before the Lord is never to be taken back. Everything that was in the waiving was to be in the life afterwards. Some get consecration and do not get the waiving. I thank the Lord for a consecration that is *forever.* People that get consecrated and find afterwards that they are not full, but are backsliding, have never been waived. A loaf of bread, a shoulder, and the breast (typical of the affections), were thus to be given in waive offering to the Lord. *Our* love is to be so wholly given to God that God can fill our souls with *perfect love,* so that we can love people even if they slap our faces, and turn us upside down and throw us in the river, so that we can love them even when we are in the river. A man may marry a woman and afterwards want to put her off and get another wife—that is devilish love. Praise the Lord for perfect love—I like that kind. That is the kind that I have had since *He married me*. I was nineteen years married before the Lord married me, and it was in the flesh, but after that it was perfect love. Let us have things in God's order; I am sick of *earthly* love.

This consecration is followed by a time of feasting. Aaron and his sons have a time! After consecration comes *feasting*. Praise the Lord I am consecrated to Him, and I feast. If the world has a big circus come around, I just feast in the Lord. This follows a true consecration. I want you to read about it in the Bible. It is real plain and it will do you good. Go down before the Lord and realize that you are a son of the High Priest, a son begotten by Jesus Christ. Down in New London, they thought I did not like my wife because I had such a burning in my soul to breathe out my life in the mission field, but when you get to this place you will realize that Jesus said, "He that loveth father or mother, husband or wife, more than Me, is not worthy of Me." I love home, I love Martha, I love everything, but somehow the Lord Almighty has my heart.

When Aaron's sons were irreverent and snatched the censer, they were killed, and lay dead by the golden altar. God expects us to be dressed in nothing but fine linen next our flesh, nothing that will cause sweat or irritation, and we will now consider the different pieces of the priest's clothing. The first one spoken of is the official robe, white and without seam, and worked in blue, purple, and scarlet, with gold *put in,* into the warp and into the woof—the eternal robe. Then there is a "curious girdle." It is a girdle of faithfulness, and has at least two turns around the body (some say more than that), enough to represent the faithfulness of the Church. "Curious!" I like that word because faithfulness is *curious.* There are only a few folks that get some of "the curious!" You can not claim the relationship of a son of Aaron unless you are wholly the Lord's, a true Levite, without any possession other than the Lord. Now follows the ouches; that is, side pieces on the shoulders, made of onyx stones and inscribed with the names of the tribes of Israel. And our names should be upon the shoulders of our great High Priest, that He might carry us in His strength, figuratively, and that we should assist in holding His official robe while He ministers. Then the breastplate. It is double, like a strong bag, and contains the Urim and Thummim, and upon the front of it the stones are attached representing the twelve tribes of Israel. It is worn upon the breast of the high priest, the breast signifying affections. The stones in this breastplate were of different kinds, no two were alike, but they all reflect the light. There were no common stones in this breastplate, they were all *gems*. You can tell whether you are a stone or not. The devil will tempt you to look at some one else and think that you are not like them and that therefore you are backsliding. But these stones did not all reflect *alike,* but every one reflects a light that God could not get along without.

Stones have hardness, color, and specific gravity; and some of them have crystalline form, and are electrical. Sanctified folks have hardness, and come up to a good polish. Electrical stones either attract or repel. We should pull everybody and everything that is good toward us, and repel that which is evil. Some people show that they need electrical properties, and they can be generated within them by the blowpipe of heat! In taking specific gravity, they weigh the stone in the air and then in water—you weigh much less in the water than in the air—and then they subtract the smaller weight from the

larger, and divide even that; and so you get it down
to a pretty small number! To make you a valuable
gem or brilliant color you must be just right; also
you might be tested as to your fusibility and your
quality of transmitting light. This latter quality
some people never have!

The ephod was the official robe made of fine linen,
embroidered with blue, purple, and scarlet, and gold
was beaten into plates and cut into wire and put
into the warp and woof of this garment. It was held
together at the shoulders by the two onyx stones
set in gold, and each bearing the names of six tribes
engraven thereon according to birth. The names of
the tribes were therefore born upon his shoulder
(strength) and his breast (affections) by means of
the breastplate. The ephod, curious girdle, and
breastplate were all made of the same material. The
priest therefore must have these garments on or the
people would not be presented before the Lord as
a memorial. Two chains from the top corners of
the breastplate were attached to rings in the shoulder
pieces which suspended the breastplate upon the
breast. The breastplate was four square, and meas-
ured about nine inches. The opening of the bag was
on the right side, and through this opening the
Urim and Thummim (lights and perfection) were
put inside, and these are typical of a finished work
after all was done and the priest clothed, and it is

typical of the baptism of the Holy Ghost. Urim and Thummim represent, too, the tribe of Levi, who were joined to the Lord and who were wholly His, having no other possession. They were not represented by any stone on the breastplate, but by this inside representation as an intercessor. See Deut. xxxiii, 8-11. "And of Levi He said, Let thy Thummim and thy Urim be with thy holy one," etc. Joseph's name was also left out of those upon the breastplate, but he was represented by Ephraim and Manasseh. There were four rows of stones and three stones in a row. First came Judah, meaning praise. His stone was a sardius; in color, red like the blood of the atonement and the wine of strong praise. He not only suffered, but was joyful in suffering, the lion of the tribe of Judah. Next, Issachar, a topaz, with rich yellow luster. Zebulon, a carbuncle, flashing redness. An emerald for Reuben. Simeon, a sapphire of pure deep blue. Gad, though overcome, was to overcome at the last, and is represented here by a diamond, which breaks or scratches all other stones. Ephraim (double faithfulness) was a ligure, glistening and variegated. Manasseh (forgetfulness), an agate, signifying the power to forget. Benjamin (son of right hand), an amethyst, a stone of great hardness and beauty, of a fine violet or purple color. Dan (judging), a beryl; the word means to break or subdue. Asher (signifying happiness), an onyx, representing the flashing forth of splendor, blessedness, and victory, the same as the shoulder stones. Napthali (thought of wrestling), a jasper, displaying various different hues, and very hard. These stones, in composition, were such that no two were alike. They all reflect the light, but each one shines in its own way; each one has its individual part to play. They were all taken out of the natural and no two were polished alike. The polishing process was not the same. Some were prepared by diamond dust, some by copper, etc. An expert can tell the stones by their sound. Some stones are combustible, some can be affected by acids, and some are unassailable by any chemical. Some are transparent, or translucent, or opaque. Some are crystalline in form and some are not, but all are *His jewels,* and we are to glorify Him in our own particular way. The ruby shines from within; the emerald borrows light from no one, while other stones are affected by the light of others, and though we may help others, yet we must all shine in the light of the Holy Ghost and come into the Holy of Holies. Gad, the conqueror, was represented by the diamond which cuts all other stones. It is of pure composition, wholly carbon, no mineral or vegetable. When destroyed by fire, it burns up so completely that it leaves no ashes. Notice the tribe of Simeon, the cruel highwayman, yet God represented him by the pure blue sapphire, and he could scratch and polish others. And how often to-day, when God takes the curse, cruelty, and wrath out of some dear one's heart, He uses them to polish others in the heavenly, like dear Simeon, and they can enter the Holy of Holies with our blessed High Priest, and shine and be with Him, O glory to God!

CHAPTER XI.

THE DAILY SACRIFICE.
(Numbers xxviii.)

EVERYTHING that is good and nice you have a place for, a *keeping* place. We will now consider the place where God desires to keep us. God wants you and me in His *keeping* place; and when you get there, and then alone, will you be kept. You will find in Deuteronomy the children of Israel were not to bring their burnt offering or heave offerings for firstfruits into *any place that they set their eye upon,* but unto God's place. The Bible clearly brings out the thought that we are His jewels. You do n't throw jewels around anywhere, but you put them in a safe place, so that when there is a fire they may be safe.

For burnt offerings there was an altar. It must be built of rough stones. A tool must not be put upon it, it would defile it. Build it of rough stones. If we will keep down where the Lord wants us (in the rough state) we will be all right! There must be no *steps* to this altar; it must be on a level with the people! The very dress of the Israelites was so arranged that they were compelled to remain upon the ground and not exalt themselves, lest they expose their nakedness. If we will walk where God wants us to we will never get exalted or proud. If we will live in the place where God chooses, He promises there to record His name. The Lord help us to look out places of His choosing! If I thought I was not in the place where God could keep me, I should do nothing until I got there. If you want to meet God, go where His name is. If I were looking for the house of a friend, I would seek it from the directions given.

God has three meeting-places: the mercy-seat, the golden altar, and the place of the continuals, or daily sacrifice. The mercy-seat was over the ark, which contained the testimony. And it is in keeping His testimony to-day that we will find sweet communion at the meeting-place with God. Communion is not a grievance. A young lady said she once read a book and she did not like it, but afterwards she fell in love with the author and then she loved his book! I do not know when I last said, "I *must* pray, I *must* go to meeting." I am through with that order. I was *glad* when I could go up (up, not down) to the house of the Lord. Some people *go* as if they were *going to the graveyard!*

The second meeting-place is the golden altar, the place of prayer. He meets us there to speak with us, but you can see right off that you must have kept His commandments to reach this sacred spot. The golden altar is by the veil, near the Ark of the Covenant, where is the mercy-seat, and whence the blood was sprinkled.

The third meeting-place is the place of continuals. When God gets us here, we will have a *perpetual* experience. The world has not yet found the secret of perpetual motion. We have it here! Praise the Lord! when one gets into the continuals we do not have to ask how he is getting along, nor inquire whether or not he has backslidden! In the place of continuals, there is an end put to any desire save the desire to *remain in this place*. Here there is a daily sacrifice, and God calls it so sweetly, "*My* offering," "*My* bread," "*My* SACRIFICE." It is a sacrifice made by fire unto the Lord that he will accept in due order. This daily sacrifice must be a *lamb,* nothing else. A lamb in the morning (nine o'clock), and a lamb in the afternoon (three o'clock). There is a meat offering of fine flour mingled with oil; and there is wine, *strong* wine, and this must be caused to be *poured out* in the holy place. When you obtain the lamb experience, the lamb spirit, you can make an offering of life, and you must pour out strong wine too in the holy place. Strong wine here stands for strong praise, not expressed with so much noise perhaps, as some one else, but just as He tells you. Shout inside *or* outside. We must all have strong wine. When we get rid of the old goat and donkey life and experience and get the lamb life, we will feel good all the time. Jesus was not only the Lamb *slain* from the foundation of the world, but when they beheld Him, *as He walked,* He was Lamb too. Lamb at nine in the morning and lamb at three in the afternoon! And on Sundays an extra sacrifice! Two lambs in the morning and two in the afternoon. Lambs follow each other; they do not all want to lead! They are always ready to be sheared; they do not murmur. And after a shearing the hair comes in again *soft,* not in bristles. Lambs are never afraid of fellowship, and they will not eat until they are at rest.

When we are in the continuals we have *plenty,* and are able to give to others.

CHAPTER XII.

FEASTS—PASSOVER AND PENTECOST.
(Leviticus xxiii.)

WE will now speak of the feasts of the Lord. There were seven in all. The word feast has two meanings: first, an appointed meeting; and second, a festival. The Sabbath is the appointed meeting of the Lord. He has the meeting, and we have the festival. Three or four of these seven feasts took place in the first part of the year, and the rest in the latter part. The first three included the Passover of unleavened bread, and the latter ones the blowing of trumpets and the feast of tabernacles, which both began and ended with a Sabbath of rest. Notice that the feast of Pentecost *preceded* the blowing of trumpets—our Pentecost must come *before the shout*. The *Passover* is described in Exodus, the book of redemption; *Pentecost* in Leviticus, the guide-book of worshipers. After leaving Egypt (where the children of Israel had been in bondage, and from which God brought them out, working in their behalf the mighty plagues, ending with the slaying of the firstborn) the Passover became the beginning of years and months to them.

The Passover lamb typifies Christ.   On the *tenth day* it was *set apart,* and on the *fourteenth day* it was *killed.*   God kept the Lamb, slain from the foundation of the world, four thousand years, before it was killed.   They sprinkled the sideposts and lintels with the blood of their lamb and the flesh was roasted with fire.   They ate it with bitter herbs in commemoration of their bondage in Egypt.   Do not forget the rock whence you were hewn, or the pit whence you were dug!   As they sat inside feasting and ready for the journey, the destroying angel passed through the land.   But when he saw the blood on the lintels, he passed by.   When that angel of death passed through the land of Egypt, they were through with the Israelites.   It was through the blood that the Israelites were set free; it is through the Blood that we obtain forgiveness of sins.   They had to eat the Passover under certain conditions; *i. e.,* with their loins girt about and their shoes on, and with staff in their hand, *in haste,* for it was the Lord's Passover.   They did not have time to bake; never more would they eat Egyptian food.   No more Egyptian bakes!   Their lives had been full of burdens and distress, but they went away well-laden with the "borrowed" jewels of silver and gold.   We must appear full of justification.

Now comes the feast of unleavened bread.   They could not eat with leaven, for leaven is a type of sin. Some people get such a work of grace done when they are justified that they do not think of getting sanctified. But the law leads us up to sanctification, for now comes the waive offering, followed by the Sabbath or preparation day, and from it they commenced to count the days, for they knew that Pentecost would come on the fiftieth day! When you come into the land, keep these feasts! From the time when this first waive offering of a sheaf of the firstfruits was made, seven Sabbaths were to be complete, and then they were to bring another offering to be waived before the Lord, consisting of two loaves of *leavened* bread; and seven lambs, one bullock, and two rams for a burnt offering, one kid for a sin offering, and two lambs of the first year for a sacrifice of peace offerings. The burnt offering was an offering of acceptance. Notice the *two* lambs for a peace offering; we have *double* peace at Pentecost.

After Pentecost was the feast of the blowing of trumpets. This took place on the first day of the seventh month. The festival of the Lord makes us glad to go unto the house of the Lord. So many promises will be fulfilled when we rightly understand these feasts. No one need lack anything. There is an abundance in the land, enough and to spare. No longer need we live a life of endurance, but we can live a life of pleasure.

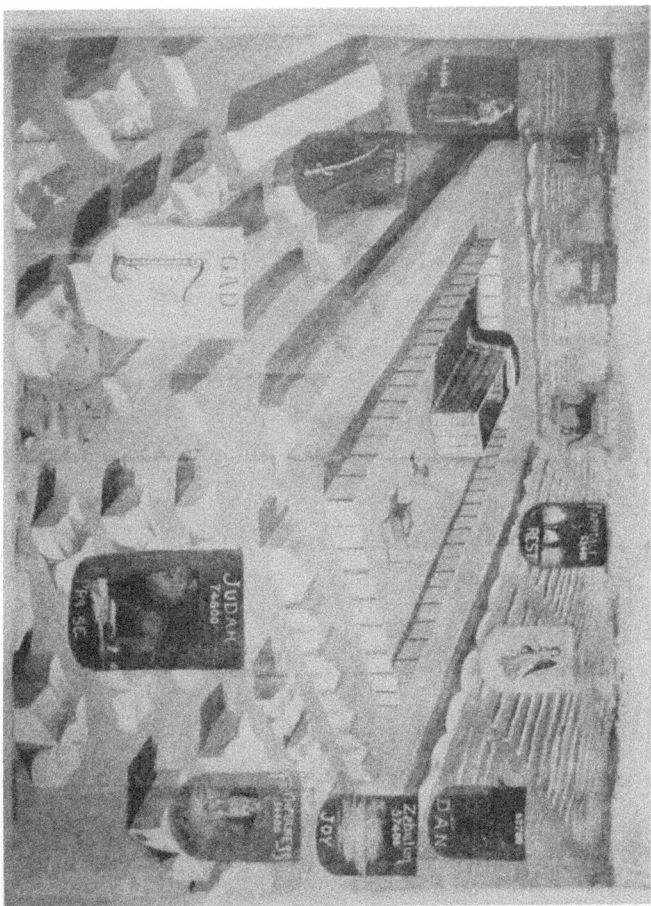

CHAPTER XIII.

THE ENCAMPMENT.

There is a natural birth and a supernatural birth. Some people hardly know where they belong, but there is a place for every one according to His Will. Before Jacob and Esau were born it was told Rebecca that the elder should serve the younger, so Rebecca tried to bring about this order of things by human means, and we find that this course resulted in one of the most terrible families that ever lived. We remember Jacob as a thief and supplanter, Rebecca helping him in the ingenuity with which he robbed Esau. When Jacob's life was in danger, Rebecca told him to flee the country and seek for himself a wife. Thereupon he went to Bethel, where he first found that there was a God. When he was free from all help and the interference of Rebecca, as he pillowed his head upon the cold ground, God revealed some things to him. After he left Bethel he journeyed on to the land of the East, where were lying three flocks of sheep waiting for the watering time, but they could not drink until Rachel (the second born) came, for she rolled the stone from the well. You can not water the

sheep until you get the second birth, for there is a
stone on the well! When Jacob saw Rachel, he
loved her, but he had to serve seven years before he
could have her. When the seven years were up,
he found he had Leah instead of Rachel, because it
was the heathen idea that the elder should wed first.
But he served seven years longer without a complaint, and married Rachel. After some strife, Joseph and Benjamin were born to Rachel *according
to God's order*. Ten children were children of the
flesh, and they proved to be a class of brigands.
The sins of the fathers are handed down to the
children of the third and fourth generations. It is
a terrible picture and it is true to-day. I pity such
cases from the bottom of my heart! The colored
man should surely bow down to the gospel, for all the
blessing and hope that there is for him is from the
gospel, and if it were not for the gospel, the woman
would be a *slave* to the man.

Let us now consider the tribes of Israel in the
order of their encampment about the tabernacle.
Judah is the first one mentioned. The birthright
really belonged to Joseph, but Judah prevailed over
his brethren and thus took the first place, and on
this account the tribe is represented by a lion. God
wants us all to be lions, not to go around devouring
everybody, but to have a shout of victory so that
when we give our testimony, everybody will feel

its force. God does not put a premium on our taking the seventh or eighth place. Every one who gets
to heaven hereafter must take a front seat, for all
the back ones have already been taken! Remember
the land where Judah dwelt was on the East, where
the new light comes. If you prevail above your
brethren and take the first place, you will get the
first light and live above other Christians.

Next comes the tribe of Issachar, the prophetic
tribe. Its symbol is that of a strong ass bowed
down between two burdens. It is *rest* in *labor*.
Rest not because the burden is heavy; but because,
though heavy, they were in a pleasant land. This
tribe could tell the other Israelites what they ought
to do. So many people want help and hardly know
what to do, but here is a tribe who knew how to
help and how to lift the burdens of others.

Now we come to Zebulon, the missionary tribe.
They dwelt by the haven for ships, that they might
go over all the globe and carry the Word of God.
They left home without a complaint, praising the
Lord that they were counted worthy. The three
tribes—Issachar, Zebulon, and Naphtali—were connected together in their missionary interest. Naphtali brought bread in abundance upon asses, camels,
and mules. The trouble with the Israel of to-day
is that she is not sending out enough missionaries.

The next in the order of the tribes is that of

Reuben, who was the firstborn. He was very un-
stable in his experience because of sin, but he was
allowed to live, though his men were to be few.

Simeon, the brother of Levi, follows Reuben.
This tribe was full of anger and self-will, and they
made it their business to cut and slash wherever
they went. Because of their anger, God scattered
them throughout all Israel and put a curse upon
them.

The next is Gad. He was a troop. If we are
looking for a fight, we will always find some one
bigger than ourselves. There is a story of two
women who used to have a fight every day. But
one day, "Bess" got salvation. The next time they
met, "Bess" never said a word, but simply looked
at the other woman with the golden crown of God's
victory upon her head. If you get a crown like that,
you will have constant victory. Keep silent; let
the crown show!

Let us now turn to the tribes of Ephraim and
Manasseh, which stand for double forgiveness—
forgiving and forgetting. Forgetting and forgiving
our brother's wrong—double forgiveness.

Next is Benjamin. He is a ravenous wolf. In
the night he takes the prey, and in the morning
divides the spoil. It makes no difference how far
he runs, he never gets tired. Benjamin was the
youngest child, and he was the beloved of the Lord,

for he dwelt between His shoulders. It is a wonderful thing to be small enough to dwell between the shoulders of God, and O what a sweetness there is in dwelling there! When the enemy comes in, just look to God, and He in turn looks the enemy in the face, and he runs.

The tribe of Dan follows Benjamin. He bites the horse's heels so that the rider falls backwards. The horse was typically a representation of Egypt, the enemy of Israel. It stands here for judgment.

The next is Asher. His bread shall be fat. He shall yield royal dainties!—a well filled life. He has a threefold blessing: he was to be acceptable to his brethren, he was to be blessed with children, and his foot was to be dipped in oil, a Holy Ghost walk!

We now come to the tribe of Naphtali, the sanctified priest. This is a wonderful tribe, represented by a hind let loose; let *loose,* not stiffly tied up! One time I landed on an island and went looking for nuts, and I heard a hind. I looked, and at first I saw something; and then I saw nothing. A sanctified preacher is a hind let loose. The mother at the birth of a little hind goes into some secluded spot, and if an enemy comes she just touches the little offspring, when only a few hours old, and it cowers down so that no one can see it. There is a peculiar enmity between the snake and the hind, and a hind will defend itself from a snake with its forefeet which are sharp and with which it pounds in rapid succession till its enemy is literally chopped to death. The Serpent will come crawling around, looking for the little hind, but the sanctified preacher understands it and chops him up! The hind's foot is nothing but bone—it is a good chopper. It is time we chopped up some of these serpents. People will complain of its not showing a loving spirit, but a *serpent* can not be treated with love. It must be chopped to death.

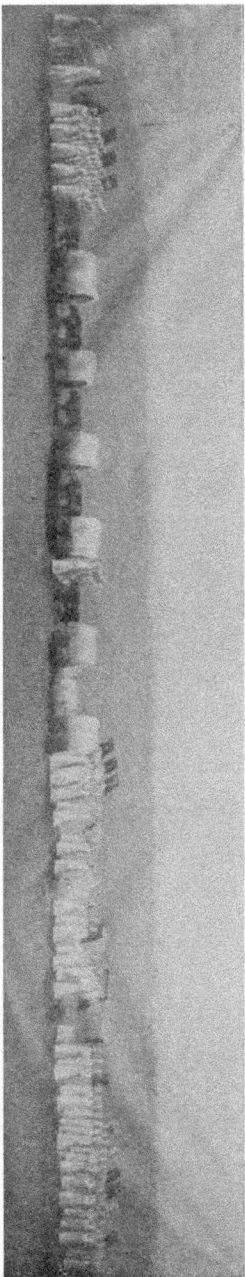
ISRAEL JOURNEYING.

CHAPTER XIV.

THE MARCH.

WE will now consider the Israelites in motion and the circumstances under which they journeyed. The cloud or the pillar of fire, the angel of God, rested above them. It served as a protection—a light, a shade, and a shield. When God spoke to them, He spoke out of the cloud. They were in a place where they could not walk in darkness, for a cloud of glory surrounded them. The first time that the pillar of fire appeared was just after the children of Israel left Egypt and were upon the edge of the wilderness.

In the fortieth chapter of Exodus we find that the tabernacle was reared in Divine order. Moses did his part, and then "a cloud covered the tent of the congregation, and the glory of the Lord filled the tabernacle." When everything is ready for the abiding of the Holy Ghost, He will come in! The *cloud* goes *over* and the *glory fills.* As they went across the Red Sea, the cloud was there to go as a shield between them and the enemies of God. The black side of the cloud was toward the enemy and the bright side was toward the children of Israel.

Some people see nothing but darkness. I passed through a red sea a thousand fathoms deep, but I went through dry shod.

At the command of Moses they journeyed, rested, and pitched their tents. We must follow the cloud, for it is never at fault. If we make a mistake, it is because our eyes are upon something else. When all preparations were made, they started out for Sinai, a journey of eleven days. It takes some people longer than that. They travel forty years, and yet find nothing in sight. The cloud served for a shade in the desert—it kept them cool. God's hand is over us; we need never get excited. "The sun shall not smite thee by day nor the moon by night." God gave to all those Israelites the same amount of light. When Moses prayed for their enemies to flee, He said, "Rise up and let thine enemies be scattered." Follow the cloud! How many move when God does not tell them to move! How many run when the wolf comes!

When the cloud lifted the priests went in and covered the furniture; then the Levites came each to carry his load. Thy had therefore to declare their pedigree that each might know just where they belonged. Each one was to take his proper place. Mr. Moody said one time a young lady came to him and said, "I wanted so much to see you that I have come to hear you preach, and have left my Sunday-school class to do so." And he said to her, "Whom did you leave your class with?" And she said, "I left it without any teacher." And he said, "Then you had better not have come. You should have staid where you belonged." So each one has an appointed place.

"For the journeyings of the camps" was one of the times for the blowing of the trumpets. Also they were to blow them in their solemn days. Blow them when death enters the family. Blow them when coal is fifteen dollars per ton! Blow them in the beginning of months. Blow them over the burnt offerings. "Must I give up *everything;* that nice house?" Blow your trumpets! Blow over your sacrifices, and over your peace offerings. Blow them when people speak well of you. It is just as necessary to blow them then as if they had spoken ill of you. Be sure there are *two* of these trumpets, and be sure you *make them for yourself;* do not borrow them. Be sure you blow them *both.* Testify to the first and second experience, for it is by the blood of the Lamb and the word of our testimony that we are to be overcomers. When you are oppressed, blow, that you may be saved from your enemies. Blow them all the time!

We will now speak of the marching order of the

7

children of Israel.   Moses went first, followed by
Aaron and his sons.   Then came the Levites, bearing
the Ark of the Testimony which was covered first
by the sacred veil, then with badger skins, and then
with blue cloth.   The camp of Judah, comprising
that tribe with that of Issachar and Zebulon, came
next.   Then the Gershonites, with two oxen and
four wagons bearing the curtains, coverings, hangings of the tabernacle, and the hangings of the court.
Then the Merarites, with four wagons and eight
oxen, and these bearing the boards, bars, pillars,
and sockets of the tabernacle, and the court pillars
and their sockets.   Then the camp of Reuben, comprising the tribes of Simeon, Reuben, and Gad.
Then the Kohathites, carrying the sacred furniture.
First, the shewbread table covered first with blue
cloth and then with *scarlet* cloth, and over all the
badger skins; then the candlestick, carried on a bar
between two men, covered with blue cloth and badger
skins.   This was followed by the golden altar and
that by the brazen laver, and as there is nothing said
about the laver being covered, it is beautiful to think
that the lesson taught is that this laver, representing
the Word of God, was left uncovered, that the Word
of God is open for all, and is so plain that the wayfar-
ing man though a fool shall not err therein.   Last of
all the furniture comes the brazen altar, covered with
a cloth of the heavenly color (blue), and over that

the badger skins, symbolic of Divine protection. Then comes the camp of Ephraim, comprising the tribes of Ephraim, Manasseh, and Benjamin. Then the camp of Dan (Dan, Asher, and Naphtali), and then the mixed multitude, which fell a-lusting. And so journeyed the children of Israel according to their tribes. See Num. iv; x, 11-36.

CHAPTER XV.

THE CLEANSING OF THE LEPER, AND THE LAWS AND TOKENS OF LEPROSY.

(Leviticus xiii and xiv.)

LEPROSY is a type of sin. Sin is of two kinds. Sin inherent we are not responsible for; sin committed we are responsible for. It was the priest who pointed out the leprosy. By *his* standard we are examined. Upon *his* examination the leprosy was pronounced and declared. Deliverance was by Divine power alone.

The leprosy was of two kinds; the dry, or scaly; and the ulcerous. Death lurks in both. The white leprosy spread through the body. The man who had it was like a walking corpse. His position was outside the camp, crying with covered lip, "Unclean!" Spiritually, this is the position of the unforgiven man. He should say, "I 'm a sinner, and unclean."

One kind of leprosy was the "fretting" leprosy. It was in the clothing, in the hair of the head, and in the home. If the priest suspects a case of leprosy, but is in doubt about the matter, he is to shut up the case for seven days. An outbreaking case could be told at once; doubtful cases would be exposed in time. You can not cover sin all the time. You might say your case was not as bad as some other person's; it is better appearing. Some have it nice and pretty; but it is there, though. Praise God, I had it *bad!* There are different kinds of explosives. Some explode with fire, and others with cold. The wife says, "Do get that chair out of the way!" The mother crosses the children, and the leprosy shows. No matter what kind it is, the priest is faithful to disclose it, be it inside fret or outside fret or home fret or head fret or clothes fret. The leprosy of the house and of the clothes is very prevalent! A house may be well painted upon the outside; but the owner may have to go to the priest and say, "It seemeth to me there is a plague in this house," and everybody in it must wash his clothes. And after that the priest examines it. He scrapes off the dust and digs out the stones. We are stones in the spiritual house; and if one becomes afflicted they must be dug out, that the disease spread not. Sometimes the mortar is so strong that the stone will break before the mortar will let go. It means something to dig out the old stone; but if any leprosy dwells in it, let us get rid of it. The reason some buildings are so torn is because the leprosy got into the stones. There is

not much of a premium upon discipline nowadays.
There are a lot of bench members. One of them
gets the leprosy, and then peddles it to some one
else. They ought to be dug out of the plaster, and
it is a terrible job to do it. The stones put in with
spiritual plaster are put there to stay. They are
never meant to get diseased, and to tear them out
sometimes means the pulling down of the whole
building. We ought to be lively stones. God means
for us to be pure. Purity is the only protection
against leprosy, and the only remedy for it. Keep
as far as you can from sin. Paul says, "While I
preach to others I fear lest I fall." Some things are
lawful, but not expedient. We can overdo in the
matter of eating. I visited once a leper colony;
but was looked carefully over first lest there might
be a scratch upon my body where I might contract
the disease. I had to be careful. It was sad to see
these people, with their own gardens providing for
themselves, cut off from civilization—outside the
camp. I keep as far from sin as I can. If God
calls me to go in the midst of it, I can go on the
Master's business. If we have the disease of leprosy (in the flesh or in the spirit), we are only
waiting for time to do its work. Even things called
blessings might become sins to us. I met a man
who tried to prove to me that eating candy was as
much of a sin as smoking was. Eating mince-pie

may be no sin in itself, yet it may bring on the dyspepsia. God has shown us some things that we must drop; we can not go that way any longer. We must be ready for God's pronunciation. Thousands are away from family relations and sanctuary privileges on account of leprosy. A "D. D." once said, "When I hear you talk about what the Lord has done for you, I almost wish I had been down in sin myself." But we do not have to drink from the devil's well in order to be able to tell what the Lord has done and can do. Many men go to the potter's field, and the ranks are filling. One hundred thousand drunkards are going down every year. Sin is the abominable thing that God hates. Let us go forward to tell of Him who can cleanse us and make us pure.

The process of cleansing was very plain. They took two living sparrows. One was to be killed in an earthen vessel over running water, and the priest was to take cedar wood and hyssop and scarlet and the living bird and dip them in the blood of the slain bird and in the running water, and to sprinkle it upon that which is to be cleansed seven times, and to let the living bird loose into the open field. Cedar wood typifies firmness, strength, and humility. By our firmness and humility, "dipped" in the precious blood of Jesus, the leprosy of sin may be banished, and our restoration be accomplished, and we may fly into the heavenly field—the open field of liberty. We may mount up on wings as eagles; we may run, and not be weary; we may walk, and not faint. When healed, his ear, thumb, and great toe were to be touched with blood and then with oil, and the rest of the oil was to be poured upon his head. When the Great Priest pronounces us leprous, we ought to bow and say, "Thank you, Lord," in court manners. We need to know it now, that we may flee to the Lamb of God that taketh away the sin of the world. We ought never to rest until He says we are *clean*. Then it is all right; and if not, it is not right.

Lord God, we thank Thee for this picture of sin and its defilement. We thank Thee for the open field and the log of oil poured on our heads. Glory to God! We thank Thee that Thou hast said, "I will, be thou clean." Help us to blaze abroad and publish the name of Him who can heal us and send us home to our dear ones and to sanctuary privileges. Amen.

CHAPTER XVI.

THE OFFERINGS.

WE will now approach the subject of offerings. There are eighteen kinds of offerings spoken of in Scripture; viz., the burnt offering, peace offering, trespass offering, heave offering, drink offering, voluntary offering, whole offering, jealousy offering, guilt offering, meat offering, sin offering, wave offering, thank offering, free-will offering, meal offering, willing offering, wood offering, and fire offering. The burnt offering signifies acceptance with God, self-dedication. The meat offering signifies life, as a Divine model; the peace offering full reconciliation, peace *with* God, and the peace *of* God; and fellowship, the believer's peace and portion. The sin offering stands for sin atoned for. The trespass offering means trespasses on God and man forgiven, and includes the thought of restitution. The drink offering is an acknowledgment of God's goodness (see 2 Sam. xxiii, 16, 17, for an example), the wine is typical of joy poured out before the Lord (Num. xxviii, 7, 8). A heave offering is something lifted up from the ground and presented on high. All the various offerings contrib-

uted to form the Tabernacle were heave offerings.
(Ex. xxv, 2-7; xxxv, 4-9.) The word "offering"
in these verses as translated in the margin means
"heave offering." The heave *shoulder* signifies the
willingness of the *heart*. All offerings must be
voluntary offerings to be accepted. The *whole*
offering must be whole to be accepted. The jealousy offering is of barley meal, without *oil* and
without *frankincense;* a memorial bringing iniquity
to remembrance. (Num. v, 14-31.) The guilt
offering (Lev. v, 1-7), a female from the flock, or
if "his hand can not reach to the sufficiency of a
lamb," he shall bring for his trespass offering two
turtle-doves, one for a sin offering and the other for
a burnt offering. (Also see Lev. v, 17; vi, 4; and
Ezra x, 19.) A wave offering (Num. xviii, 20) is
waved before the Lord. There was the wave shoulder and the wave breast and the handful of wheat
from the field, and they were to be given to the high
priest and to his sons by reason of the anointing by
an ordinance forever. "All the best of the oil and all
the best of the wine and the wheat, them have I
given thee, and whatsoever is first ripe in the land,
everything devoted in Israel shall be thine; it is a
covenant of salt forever before the Lord unto thee
and to thy seed with thee. Thou shalt have no inheritance in their land, neither shalt thou have any

part among them. I am thy part and thy inheritance among the children of Israel." We are to offer a thank offering to God continually for His "unspeakable gift." (See Ezek. xliii, 20-27; Amos v, 22; Luke ii, 28, 29.) The free-will offering is mentioned in Lev. xxii, 18-21; Deut. xii, 6; and Psa. cxix, 108. Notice that it was to be offered in the place which the Lord your God should choose out of all your tribes to put his name there, even unto His habitation thither they should come. The psalmist prays God to accept the free-will offering of his mouth. The meal offering is allied with the other offerings, especially the meat offering. The willing offering was anything offered willingly from the heart. (Ex. xxv, 2; see Judg. v, 2.) There was a time when they blessed all the men that willingly offered themselves to dwell at Jerusalem. Lots were cast in regard to those who were to bring the wood offering at the times appointed for the continued fire. (See Neh. x, 34; and xiii, 31.) There was also a fire offering. As we are on the altar we are fire offerings. Fire means light and heat; it *tries* and *purges* metals; it *burns* "wood, hay, and stubble." It is a symbol of the holiness and justice of God. Our God is a "consuming fire." It is the baptism of the Holy Ghost and fire, which enlightens, purifies, and sanctifies. There was food for the fire, and we are food for God's fire, an acceptable offering of a sweet savor. The wine offering is the same as the drink offering.

Genesis is the book of beginnings. Exodus, the book of departure (Then Moses said, Let my people go, that we may go three days' journey in order to worship). Leviticus is the guide-book of worship. It is the *third* book, the book of resurrection life! The word means to exhale (or cause to ascend) odor. Numbers is the guide-book to travelers. Deuteronomy is the book of Christian experience. Joshua the book of conquest. The only approach for acceptable worship is by way of the brazen altar; it is God's chosen place, and is sought with a definite object. All furnished the wood for its sacred and continual fire.

The offerings of individuals were many. And there were public offerings daily, weekly, monthly, and yearly. Some were for acceptance, and were *inside* the gate; some were for sin, and were *outside* the gate. Some were free-will offerings; others were obligatory. In an offering there must be no leaven, the type of sin; no honey, the type of natural goodness or sweetness of the flesh; but *always salt,* meaning truth or grace. Salt was a pledge of fidelity in friendship. To eat bread and salt together expressed a league of mutual unity. On the other hand, the Persian term for traitor is faithlessness to salt. (See Lev. ii, 13. See the significance of a covenant of salt as an inviolable engagement in Num. xviii, 19, and 2 Chron. xiii, 5.) It must be offered in the place of service. "Whatsoever man there be of the house of Israel, or of the strangers that sojourn among you, that offereth a burnt offering or sacrifice, and bringeth it not unto the door of the Tabernacle of the congregation to offer it unto the Lord, even that man shall be cut off from among his people."

The burnt offering is the highest sacrifice in Scripture. The law of it is given in Lev. vi, 8-13. It is the burnt offering because of the burning upon the altar *all night unto the morning!* Upon this occasion the priest wears a peculiar dress of fine white linen garments. It is an ascending offering, and the fire of the altar shall be burning in it. The word for burning used here is only found in this chapter. In the sin and trespass offering the skin is burnt; but in the burnt offering it is given to the priest. Noah's offerings when he came out of the ark were of this character (Gen. viii, 20-22), and the Lord smelled (margin) a savor of rest; and the Lord said in his heart, I will not again curse the ground any more for man's sake. Abraham's offering was of this character when he "offered" Isaac. When this offering was made for the priest and his sons, they identified themselves with the victim by putting their hands upon its head, and its blood was sprinkled round about and upon the horns of the golden altar, and poured at the bottom of it. In the ram of consecration, notice that in its natural life it had only one tone to his voice like that of bleating; but after death from his inwards were secured seven large strings for lute strings, and some small ones for harp strings. Its horns were used for trumpets, its leg bones for flutes, its skin for a drumhead, its wool for the covering of the pomegranates on the eternal robe to ring the bells of the high priest; the whole to produce one sound that brings out the complete note of entire consecration to God.

CHAPTER XVII.

THE BURNT, MEAT, AND PEACE OFFER-
ING.

In the burnt offering the greater the size of the victim the longer for it to be consumed to ashes, and the more the fat the hotter the fire. As in the case of the bullock (if of the flock sheep or goats), it was killed on the north side of the camp, where was the tribe of Dan (judgment), Asher (final victory), and Naphtali (the tribe of the sanctified preachers, God's ministers who are a flame of fire), before the Lord and the priest was to sprinkle the blood and cut the body into his pieces and lay these in order upon the altar on the wood and on the fire, his legs (our walk) and his inwards (our affections) after their being washed. God has "an order," and we must meet it to be accepted. But in case of poverty (having no possessions of this world), there might be offered a turtle-dove or young pigeon. A dove does not walk like the previous victim, but in its purity, power to fly, is symbolic of a heavenly creation and life; nevertheless it goes upon the altar the same as the other, and is consumed to ashes. The offerer has not much to do. He does not have to kill himself or his offering in this case; but the priest does it for him. He (the priest) wrings off the head and sheds the blood upon the altar, and it is an offering of sweet savor unto the Lord made by fire, the same as in the other cases; but the smaller we are the quicker the work, and the less room and care required!

The priest shall put on linen garments and take up the ashes and lay them beside the altar eastward, where they will receive the first light; then the priest, putting off those garments and putting on clean ones, shall carry the ashes forth outside the camp into a clean place, where they are kept. And so he keeps us with Him, outside the camp, bearing His reproach, crucified with Christ.

The meat offering was a food offering. It comes after the burnt offering. There was one kind of fine flour (our life after forgiveness), with oil (Holy Ghost) mingled, and another of fine flour, with oil poured. There was to be no leaven (the secret working of sin), no honey (good self life); but frankincense (typical of Christ) and salt (typical of truth or grace). The law of this offering is found in Lev. vi, 14-24. Notice the priest shall take all the frankincense, not part. It shall be burnt upon the altar for a sweet savor, even the memorial of it, unto the Lord. The remainder shall be eaten by the sons of Aaron the priest. So we shall have to be anointed priests unto God to partake of this meat offering. Every one that toucheth it shall be holy.

The peace offering is of the herd or flock, male or female, without blemish before the Lord. The offerer shall lay his hands upon it, making it identical with himself. The law of this offering is found in Lev. vii, 11-36. There are two kinds of peace; there is peace with God and the peace of God, and this latter perfect peace is spoken of in the margin as "peace, peace," or double peace. One is the first experience; the other is a second work. We find them both brought out in the peace offering. First the blood is sprinkled, for there is no peace without the blood; also the fat that covers the inwards, and the kidneys and the fat that is on them, which is by the flank that holds the inwards and connects the foreleg and hindleg and the caul (margin, midriff), that which divides the upper from the lower inwards shall be taken away, and this shall be a separate offering from the rest of the body, a double offering, a double peace inside and outside.

And then there is a food part of the offering, the rump taken off hard by the backbone. The backbone is the foundation of things. This peace is to be built up from the foundation. We are to have peace everywhere and on all sides. And if the offering be offered for a thanksgiving, then he shall offer with the sacrifice of thanksgiving unleavened cakes

8

mingled with oil, and unleavened cakes anointed with oil. Be careful for nothing; but in everything by prayer and supplication with *thanksgiving* let your requests be made known unto God, and the peace of God which passeth all understanding shall keep your hearts and minds through Jesus Christ. The unleavened cakes, mingled with oil, are the first work; the unleavened wafers anointed with oil, and cakes mingled with oil, of fine flour *fried,* are the perfect peace, and speak of the suffering foretold in the words, "They that live godly in Christ Jesus shall suffer persecution." And the flesh of the sacrifice of his peace offerings for thanksgiving shall be eaten the same day that he offereth his sacrifice. He shall not leave any of it until the morning, but must hasten forward to the second offering which shall be eaten the same day, and on the morrow the remainder of it shall be eaten, and on the third day the remainder of the flesh of the sacrifice shall be burnt with fire. The second peace continues until the third, the resurrection or manifestation day, when it shall be burnt with fire. If any of the flesh of the sacrifice be eaten on the third day it shall not be accepted; it shall be an abomination, and the soul that eateth of it shall bear its iniquity. While it is continued peace, it must be new or fresh. No one that toucheth any unclean man or beast or abominable thing shall eat the flesh of this sacrifice; if

he eat it with his uncleanness upon him he shall be
cut off. The offerer with his own hands brings this
offering.   It is to be made by fire.   The breast
(affections) shall be waved for an offering before
the Lord, and shall then belong to Aaron and his
sons.   The right shoulder (strength) shall be an
heave offering, and belong to the officiating priest.
"For the wave breast and the heave shoulder have I
taken of the children of Israel from off the sacrifices
of their peace offerings, and have given them unto
Aaron the priest and unto his sons by a statute forever from among the children of Israel.   This is
the portion of the anointing of Aaron, and of the
anointing of his sons out of the offerings of the
Lord made by fire, in the day when he presented
them to minister unto the Lord in the priest's office,
which the Lord commanded to be given them of the
children of Israel, in the day that he anointed them,
by a statute forever throughout their generations,
. . . which the Lord commanded Moses in Mt.
Sinai, in the day that He commanded the children
of Israel to offer their oblations unto the Lord in
the wilderness of Sinai."   We are the anointed
priests, and eat peace. We have the high priest's
blessing in the peace offering.

CHAPTER XVIII.

THE SIN AND TRESPASS OFFERINGS.

THE first offering brought by Moses was a bullock for the sin offering. In the original language the word "offering" does not appear, connected with the various sacrifices, so that it would read, and there was brought "the bullock—the sin." And the original force of the words "laid their hands on" sometimes means *"leaning heavily"* (upon the head of the offering). The priest had previously become acquainted with the sin offering at the time of his consecration. Every sacrifice which had been presented to God from Abel's time down had been a burnt sin offering. There was a sin offering for the priest, for the congregation, for the ruler, and for the common people. If a priest that is anointed do sin, "let him (publicly confessing his sin) bring a bullock unto the door of the Tabernacle and lay his hand upon its head and kill the bullock, and let the priest that is anointed dip his finger in the blood and sprinkle of it seven times before the Lord before the veil of the sanctuary," and some of the blood shall be put on the horns of the golden altar, and the rest poured

out at the bottom of the brazen altar, and the priest
shall be cleansed and made right to intercede with
God at the golden altar of prayer. This is the sin
offering for the anointed priest; but notice that the
body of the victim offered is treated the same as in
his original offering of consecration at the brazen
altar, for there was a thorough examination and a
minute offering, the same as the peace offering of
the inside fat and kidneys, the skin, flesh, head, legs,
inwards, and dung, the *whole* bullock, and it must
be carried without the camp to the place of ashes,
the clean place, and with all the old life figuratively
destroyed he begins anew.

In the sin offering for the congregation the elders
lay their hands on the offering when the sin is
known, and sacrifice is made the same as in the
case of the priest, and the priest shall make an atonement for them, and it shall be forgiven them. This
is the offering for the sin of ignorance for the whole
congregation when the thing be hid from the eyes
of the assembly, and they have done somewhat
against any of the commandments of the Lord concerning things which should not be done, and are
guilty. We are to have a care over one another,
and not to suffer our neighbor ignorantly to sin.

When the ruler (prince, noble, head of family
or tribe) hath sinned, *"and it come to his knowledge"*—we see by this expression what a rare thing

God expected sin to be, and how far God expected
his children to live from it—he shall bring his offering, a kid of the goats, a male without blemish, and
the priest shall take of the blood of the sin offering
with his finger, and put it upon the horns of the
altar of burnt offering, and shall pour out his blood
at the bottom of the same. The horns represent
power, the *golden* altar is not touched in this offering, nor was it in the case of the assembly; but the
consecration, by means of the brazen altar, must be
made all right.

And if any one of the common people sin through
ignorance, he shall bring his offering, a kid of the
goats, a *female* without blemish (signifying the
Church, the bride) or a female lamb without blemish. The lamb is mild and pure, like the life God
expected them to live. And the priest shall make
atonement, and it shall be forgiven him. It is prob-
able that the law of trespass and sin offering were
one. In the place of the burnt offering shall they
kill the trespass offering, and all the fat that is on
it and the caul above the liver with the kidneys
shall be taken away, and the priest shall burn them
upon the altar, and every *male* among the priests
shall eat it (it seems that some among the priests
were females), and in all cases (with this excep-
tion) shall it be eaten in the holy place.

The trespass offering teaches us the necessity of

a close walk with God. We are not to hear the voice of swearing nor to touch any unclean thing, be it of man or beast. Even if it be done in ignorance it must be confessed, and an offering must be made unto the Lord, a female from the flock, a kid or a lamb. But if he be not able to bring these he can bring two turtledoves or two young pigeons, "and he shall bring his trespass offering unto the Lord for his sin which he hath sinned," *unto the Lord,* not to a priest nor to the Virgin Mary. God alone can forgive sins, though the priest can help by "wringing off the head from the neck; but he shall not divide it asunder. This offering does not divide, but keeps us. He shall sprinkle the blood upon the side of the altar where all can see it, and the rest he shall wring out at the bottom of the altar, and he shall offer the other bird for a burnt offering according to the manner or ordinance, and the priest shall make atonement for his sins, and it shall be forgiven him. But if he be not able to bring the turtledoves or pigeons, he shall bring a tenth part of an ephah (about 3 quarts) of fine flour; but he shall put no oil upon it, neither any frankincense thereon, for it is a sin offering, and when we have sinned there is no *oil nor frankincense about us.* And a handful of this shall be burnt for a memorial, and atonement shall be made for him.

And the Lord spake unto Moses, saying, if a

soul commit a trespass and sin through ignorance in "the holy things of the Lord"—a ram shall be brought with thy estimation by shekels of silver, and he shall make amends for the harm that he hath done in the holy thing, and he shall add the *fifth part* thereto (Benjamin's portion). How sure we must be that we trespass not in ministration of the Lord! God's eye is upon us all the time, and we should take our shoes from off our feet, for the ground upon which we stand is holy ground.

CHAPTER XIX.

THE NAZARITE VOW AND HIGH PRIEST BLESSING.

(Numbers vi.)

THE Nazarite vow means separation. No character brought such wonderful things to pass as the Nazarite did. Real separation to God always brings things crosswise with sin. We must walk, in a sense, above the general order of things. It is, indeed, *individual* separation unto God. The question is not whether we will please our loved ones, or whether they will walk *with us;* but we must go to heaven alone and enjoy it alone. During the time of separation the Nazarite was not allowed to drink any wine or strong drink. Wine means mirth or joy. God expects us to have the joy of the Lord for our strength—not hilarious joy, but the supernatural. If we have this joy we are equal to every emergency, and there is no failure.

We now come to the locks of hair, which typify consecration. Our head, and in fact our whole body, must be consecrated unto the Lord. If we are crippled in the spiritual body, we will be shorn of spiritual strength. As we go on in the separate life,

God expects us to live so Christ-like that no one can condemn us. All the days of our separation are holy unto the Lord. It will be a life in which people can implicitly trust us at *any time* and in *any place*. We must not make ourselves unclean for father or mother or sister or brother. How many people lose years of separation, because they have broken their vow of "holiness unto the Lord." Your life used to be one of holy separation; but now you no longer enjoy sweet communion with the Master. Can you be restored? Yes, by the offering of the two turtledoves! yet you can not but recall those days with bitterness. Lord, help us to make up the lost days!

Let us now speak of the *turtledoves*. They have no gall; they have no ingenuity or cunning. One peculiar feature is that they are *always* mated, and are especially noted for their love for one another. One is a type of the Holy Ghost; the other a type of the Church. When the Church drifts into worldliness and formality, the Holy Ghost mourns incessantly for it. As the dove's eye reflects and sees afar off, so we should look to the land far away, even toward the eternal city. Once a young married man was called to the Philippines to fight for his country. He left his wife at home; but finally she said that she must go there too. No one could persuade her to stay at home. She simply must go, for her life was separated unto her husband; apart from him she was wretched. How much more important it is that our lives be so given up to the Holy Ghost that we can not endure separation from Him! Samson was shorn of his strength because he came in contact with a "dead body." His locks were shaven from his head, and when he was shorn he had no more strength than an ordinary man. Then his eyes were put out and his spiritual vision was blurred. They made all manner of sport of him. People point their finger at the backslider now, and say, "Is that the one who used to have so much power; is he the one who professed to be saved and sanctified?" God, help us to keep clear of dead bodies!

We have some instances in the Bible of lives that were separated unto the Lord. Samuel's life was one of holy separation, even from his mother's womb. He died a natural death (after Israel had backslidden). When God puts a Nazarite into the field he stays there until there is no more use for him. As Daniel went through the lion's den and the three Hebrew children through the furnace, they kept their vow and stood true to God. Separation puts holy steel into us. When we go through the furnace experience, the form of the Fourth is with us. The true Nazarite meets tests without a flinch. John the Baptist was another true Nazarite, for he lived the separated life in the wilderness. Because he rebuked sin in that wicked, passionate damsel he was beheaded. God, help us to rebuke sin when we see it, and live a life separated unto Him! At the end of the Nazarite vow was the high priest blessing.

Dear readers, let us then see that we make Him a sanctuary, that He may dwell with us, yea *in us*. And let us see that we make it in all things according to the pattern shown us in the mount. Let us take upon us the true Nazarite vow, for in so doing we shall individually find the high priest's blessing to rest upon us, and let its sweet benediction therefore be our closing words: The Lord bless thee and keep thee: the Lord make His face shine upon thee, and be gracious unto thee: the Lord lift up His countenance upon thee, and give thee peace! Amen.

ADDENDUM.

Symbolism of numbers in the tabernacle and its service. "Destroy . . . not (*the cluster*) for a blessing is in it!"

ONE.

There was one sanctuary (a place set apart), one tabernacle, one high priest, one ark of the covenant, one law, one pot of manna, one holy of holies, one holy place, one court, one month and one year (in the signification of the first month and the first year) one prominent " first " day of creation, one bride and one bridegroom, one Lord and one faith and one baptism. In the offering of the prince's at the dedication of the altar, from the first to the twelfth day, there was: One silver charger (dish) one spoon of gold full of incense, one lamb, one ram and one kid, together with two oxen, five rams, five he-goats, and five lambs of the *first* year, and all this after the high priest blessing.

TWO (Unity.)

Two places in the sanctuary, two cherubim, two staves, two persons in service (the high priest and the manifestation of God's presence), two sacred manifestations of fires (the fire on the altar lit from heaven, and the shekinah glory), two rows of shew bread, two Levites carrying the candlestick, two tenons in the boards and two pieces of silver in foundation, two animal and two cloth coverings, two rings to twine together and two rings for the staves, the second day in creation, and the second year and the second month, two oxyx stones on the shoulders of the high priest, two changes of raiment, two wave loaves at feast of Pentecost, two silver trumpets, a wagon for two princes, two principal workmen. In creation *two*. Man made in God's image. We will come and make our abode with him. One-ness is essential to unity.

THREE.

Third day resurrection or manifestation day. Trinity
was manifested in the ark of the covenant.* There were
three kinds of light, three pieces of furniture in the holy
place, three colors in the doors, three golden sides of the
sanctuary, three branches in candlestick and three orna-
mentations under the branches. There was a *third* day,
and with it dry land and fruitage, and three stones in the
rows of the breast-plate.

FOUR, (the Number of Humanity and Dispersion.)

Four corners, four pillars of gate and veil and four colors
in veil, four sides, four coverings, four garments for the
high priest, four wagons of the Merarities, four oxen of the
Gershonites, four rows in the breast-plate, four sides in the
crystalline form, four rivers in Eden, four seasons of the
year, the lights created on the fourth day, four compounds
of the holy incense, four golden rings of boards, ark of
covenant, shewbread and brazen altar and in shaft of candlestick. Sometimes four signifies completion as in four
corners.

FIVE (is the Number of Imperfection or Incompleteness.)

There were five curtains in the linen and goat's hair covering, five pillars for the door, five bars in the side of the
sanctuary, five cubits in the height of the curtain of the
outer court, and the pillars are five cubits apart (and twice
five cubits.) The fifth day in creation, the five shekels for
poll-tax of first-born, the five high priests, in the fifth year
the fruit of the tree was eaten, in keeping rank five persons
were "harnessed" abreast, the portion of Benjamin (the
"right-hand" son) was five times that of the others.

SIX (signifies Toil.)

Six goat's hair curtains, six loaves of bread, six branches
in candlestick, six days to toil in gathering manna, six names
on each shoulder of the high priest, six-faced cube, six covered wagons, six cities of refuge.

---

* The tables of testimony, the gold pot of manna, and Aaron's rod
that budded.

SEVEN (signifies Perfection.)

On the seventh day they ceased from labor, the day of rest; seven pieces of tabernacle furniture, seven days in consecration, seven days to be clean from contact of dead body, seven times seven for feast of unleavened bread.

EIGHT.

Eighth day (service) equals the new or feasting day.

NINE.

Trinity of trinity, cube.

TEN (is the Number of Man's Side and of Trial.)

Ten fine linen curtains, Passover 10th day of month, also the day of atonement, Ten Commandments, length of the boards and height of the pillars ten cubits.

ELEVEN (lack of Complete Organization.)

Found in goat's hair covering, and in eleven days' journey from Horeb to Kadesh.

TWELVE.

Twelve breastplate stones, twelve camps, twelve tribes, twelve princes, twelve rods, twelve loaves of bread.

www.ingramcontent.com/pod-product-compliance
Lightning Source LLC
Chambersburg PA
CBHW021153020426
42331CB00003B/39